RASCAL

MAKING A DIFFERENCE BY BECOMING
AN ORIGINAL CHARACTER

CHRIS BRADY

Foreword by Orrin Woodward

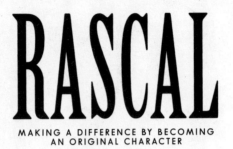

RASCAL

MAKING A DIFFERENCE BY BECOMING
AN ORIGINAL CHARACTER

CHRIS BRADY

Second Edition, March 2012

Published by:
Obstaclés Press, Inc.
4072 Market Place Dr.
Flint, MI 48507

Cover design and layout by Norm Williams
Comic illustrations by Sean Catron

To my children:
May you remain the Rascals you already are!

"Sometimes even if he has to do it alone, and his conduct seems to be crazy, a man must set an example, and so draw men's souls out of their solitude, and spur them to some act of brotherly love, that the great idea may not die."
- The mysterious visitor to Father
Zossima in The Brothers Karamazov

"To be nobody but yourself in a world that's doing its best to make you somebody else, is to fight the hardest battle you are ever going to fight. Never stop fighting."
- E. E. Cummings

"All might be free if they valued liberty, and defended it as they should."
- Samuel Adams

"One should either not lift a finger against the mighty, or, if one does, one must do it thoroughly."
- Rinaldo deglie Albizzi

Acknowledgments

Every book is a team effort, and without a great group of people around me this one would never have seen the light of day. I am, as usual, particularly indebted to my wife Terri, whose patience and partnership have meant everything to me. She painstakingly organized the Assessment Test in this book, checking and adjusting until it was right. My long-time business partner and friend Orrin Woodward was gracious enough to offer to write the Foreword, and I deeply appreciate his kind words therein. Additionally, his input and suggestions made this book much better than it would have been. I would also like to thank Rob Hallstrand and the marvelous staff at Obstacles Press, Inc. for monumental achievements behind the scenes. You have all done an amazing job! Also, Bill Rousseau has been a joy to work with and a true professional. As usual, Norm Williams has done a spectacular job putting my thoughts and visions into graphics and layouts. I will never know exactly how you pull it off. Much gratitude is also due my assistant Doug Huber for not only covering the bases, but also anticipating what I need before I even realize it. Also, to my friends and business partners on the Policy Council of the Team, Tim and Amy Marks, Bill and Jackie Lewis, Claude and Lana Hamilton, Dan and Lisa Hawkins, and George and Jill Guzzardo, thanks for embodying what this book is all about. You are Rascals, all!

Thanks also to my parents, Jim and Gayle Brady, whose example continues to guide me with my own children: I couldn't have asked for better parents. Also to my brother Pat Brady, who finds all kinds of little ways to help me out all the time. And finally and most importantly, I wish to give all glory to my Lord and Savior Jesus Christ. Everything I have and will ever accomplish is by His grace.

Table of Contents

Foreword

Rascal? Who are you to be calling me names? But that is exactly what every great achiever is in life. Rascals are willing to step out of line and pursue their own dreams, not conform to the wishes of the masses. What is it that separates the Rascals from the rest of humanity? Chris Brady's new book will reveal that and much more.

I have known Chris Brady since I was 17 years old and have been a business partner and close friend for 15 plus years. As I read his captivating book on Rascals, I saw so many parallels between the characters described and Chris that I have named him *Honorary First Rascal*. Rascals fear insignificance more than they fear peer pressure; they fear losing more than they fear change; they fear endless talk more than dangerous actions. I believe that everyone has inside of them a rascal, but it has been buried by endless, mind-numbing conditioning to be part of the herd.

Let me share just a few highlights of Chris Brady's life as an example of rascality. Chris grew up in a middle class family with supportive parents who taught their two boys that anything was possible in life. Chris bought into this principle and pursued his passion for racing motorcycles to a competitive level, even though he started at the late age of 16. From this early success, he parlayed his work ethic into a sponsorship with General Motors and a degree at the prestigious GMI Engineering & Management Institute (now Kettering University). Chris graduated at the top of his class and went on to obtain his Masters at Carnegie Mellon University, even conducting his thesis in Japan. With all of these credentials for success behind him, you would think he would have followed the traditional route and climbed the corporate ladder. Everything certainly seemed to indicate that he should.

All of this changed when he went to a Michael Dell seminar and learned from a billionaire that many of tomorrow's future leaders would be those who could master the art of building communities that drive traffic to on-line sites. Being the Rascal that he is, Chris put all of his efforts and know-how to work, leaving his corporate job, and putting everything on the line to develop his leadership skills and systems understanding to help found the TEAM. The rest, as they say, is history. Hundreds of thousands of people in community and millions of dollars of revenue later and a lifestyle that is incomprehensible to non-rascals, Chris and his lovely wife Terri have traveled the world with their four talented children. With multiple best selling books including a *Wall Street Journal #1* Best Seller: *Launching a Leadership Revolution*, I would say Chris has broken out of the herd.

What made the difference? Was it just sheer talent? Luck, by being in the right spot at the right time? Connections? God's Providence? The Bradys would certainly agree they have been blessed, but I believe this book spells out many of the keys of the Bradys Rascal-like success. If I were to boil it down into one sentence, I would say Rascals have the courage to pursue their own dreams. Chris knew what he wanted and pursued it with a singular focus against opposition, against the norms, against the setbacks until success finally surrendered its secrets. In life, you either hate losing so much that you are willing to change or you hate changing so much that you are willing to lose. Rascals cannot stand the thought of surrendering their dreams, so instead surrender their comforts in pursuit of their destiny.

I am proud to strongly recommend this book to all who dare to dream and hunger for significance in life. Chris doesn't promise *easy* when you step up to the Rascal plate, but he does promise *worth it*! Get reading and find out that everything you need to be a Rascal has been inside of you all along.

Orrin Woodward
Top Ten International Association of Business Leaders
HR's Top 100 Leadership Blogger

Preface

Some things are easier to demonstrate than they are to explain: easier caught than taught. The concept of a unique type of person, affectionately called a *Rascal* in these pages, is a prime example. In this book, we will consider the characteristics of Rascals, noting their greatness and analyzing their behaviors. As we do so, it will be most illustrative to simply observe some representative individuals as a way to shine light on the whole concept.

What you may notice while reviewing this gallery of Rascals is the large range of background, circumstances, age, gender, and race they collectively represent. These things, being external, have nothing to do with the concept. Being a Rascal is an outpouring of who a person is on the inside. It is a spirit of willfulness and strength, a dynamic force that drives one forward toward a unique path and contribution. It is character in motion, originality in broad relief, uniqueness for the sake of being true to one's self and one's cause. It is authenticity in courageous display. It is life lived on purpose and for a purpose.

Introduction

As an adolescent, Lakota warrior-leader Crazy Horse witnessed the peacemaker Conquering Bear being gunned down in cold blood by American soldiers. The warriors on the scene attacked and killed the soldiers in self-defense. Shortly thereafter, Crazy Horse rode upon the remnants of a village massacred in a retaliatory raid by the soldiers. He found mutilated bodies and other atrocities. Still in the formative portion of his youth, Crazy Horse was deeply affected, and subsequently had a vivid and life-like night dream. It was of a warrior emerging from a calm lake on a horse of changing colors. Hanging behind the warrior's left ear was a reddish-brown stone. His face was painted with yellow lightning, his chest with blue hailstones. As the warrior rode, he was impervious to the bullets and missiles of his enemy. Behind him were storm clouds full of thunder and lightning. But also behind him were his own people, who rose up to pull him down.

The Lakota believed that the Thunder Beings (*Wakinyan*) that lived in the storm clouds of the west were among the strongest of all spirits. Anyone who dreamed of them was expected to walk a different path than the rest of the "normal" people; the path of the *Heyoka* or *wakan witkotkoka*, meaning "crazy in a sacred way." According to Joseph M. Marshall III, "A Heyoka was a walking contradiction, acting silly or even crazy sometimes, but generally expected to live and act contrary to accepted rules of behavior. In doing so a Thunder Dreamer sacrificed reputation and ego for the sake of the people."

Crazy Horse was the very embodiment of the Heyoka. Quiet and reserved, he avoided the boasting sessions of battlefield tales. As a loner he had the kind of humility requisite in the "reluctant leader." Haunted and prodded by his youthful vision, he carried a serious sense of purpose and determination to serve his people. He was steely and seemingly untouchable in battle. In his prime, Crazy Horse and his fellow braves out-fought two of the United States Army's top commanders. While other respected Lakota leaders capitulated and brought their people in to the government reservations, Crazy Horse fought on. Not until his ammunition was nearly spent and he had no way to protect the women and children did he reluctantly lead his followers to the agency. Ultimately, he was literally stabbed in the back by his own people and thereafter ascended into legend.

Crazy Horse was one of a kind. He walked his own path. He followed his own inner voice. He was courageous and brave. He stood for good as he knew it. He followed his convictions. He was nobody's fool. Fulfilling his "crazy sacred" calling, he sacrificed not only his reputation and ego for the sake of his people, but his very life. In short, he had the character to be a character.

Doesn't it seem that the most interesting characters in a novel, play, or history tale are the ones who walk their own walk, go their own way, and seem to resist the compliancy pressures of the world? These individuals may have some obvious foibles; they may not always be saints; but they are *interesting*; they are *real!* In a sense, they are a *brand* all their own.

One such person was a relative of mine. He called himself the *Rascal Frenchman* and opened a barbershop by the same name. His cottage in the woods by a lake, the Northern Pike fish-heads nailed to a tree, the putting green on his deck, the trees growing up through it because he didn't want to cut them down, and his dog named Barf-Barf will never be forgotten. He had funny jokes and great stories, and he even wrote a novel once. Most memorable, however, was his funeral. Most of us water-skied all morning before finally making our way to the small service. And just as the eulogy was beginning, someone popped the lid on a "cold one" very loudly in the back of the room.

Some of these things are interesting, some, not so flattering. Together, though, these details make him stand out from the crowd as a *character*. He was certainly an individual, doing things his own way and living a unique life. And his creative brand name, *The Rascal Frenchman*, painted on the door of his old brown pickup truck, is the inspiration for the title of this book.

In these pages, we will certainly not be romanticizing the hedonistic lifestyle. We won't be talking about nonconformity as a value in and of itself. Rather, we will be investigating the concepts involved in living a life *on purpose*, carving one's own path, and having the courage to live as only you and God see fit. In short, we will be examining what it takes, what it means, and what results from having the character to become an original. And though we are taking inspiration from the original Rascal Frenchman for the terminology, the representative character will be seen to be a bit more like Crazy Horse.

It takes character to be different. It takes character to stand apart from the masses for legitimate, purposeful reasons. It takes character to be who God called you to be without succumbing to the pressures of others and their ideas of who you should be and how you should live. For those who embody this concept and live a truly authentic life, we will assign the name *Rascal*.

Webster's defines a rascal as "a mean, unprincipled, or dishonest person." The second definition is "a mischievous person or animal." In our usage of the term Rascal, we will be leaving behind most of Webster and crafting a definition of our own. The only thing we may take along is an aspect of mischief.

The idea of classifying a group of people based upon their behavior and modifying an age-old word definition to do so is not without its perils. Some may assign a bit too much malice to the term Rascal. More appropriately for our modification of the definition, however, would be a consideration of *The Little Rascals* of

black and white television fame. They weren't scoundrels or crimi-
nals, but good-hearted children full of mischief and curiosity, pre-
cociousness and pluck. The result was a very entertaining clump
of individuals. For our usage, this picture will be useful to keep in
mind.

Also, the behavior of our new classification of people is very di-
verse. Some of the featured Rascals demonstrated their particular
quality worthy of our mention in only a moment's action. Others were a showcase for the very idea itself over the course of their
entire lives, and obviously, the remainder fall somewhere between
these two extremes. Regardless of their time on the stage of our
notice, they were chosen for these pages because they embody a
special quantity of force; a personality and authenticity driven by
courage and principle; a dedication to their over-arching sense of
justice; and a behavior most-becoming of our new definition for
the old word Rascal.

Once reviewing the attributes of Rascals, seeing the colorful and
often exciting lives of some of history's most notorious examples,
and purveying the principles of living the type has in common, a
definition for the term won't even be required. Instead, readers will
get a clear idea about their own level of "Rascalinity" and will be
able to identify Rascals in their own circles of friends. This will be
aided further by the Test of Rascalinity to be found in Chapter 6; a
fun, if not scientific, self-evaluation. Some readers may prefer beginning there and obtaining an advance look at their own personal
level of Rascalinity before diving into the rest of the material.

The purpose of this book, however, extends beyond creative
classifications and clever word definitions, and although it is full of
principles for self growth and personal achievement, it is broader
than that in scope. It was written as a wake-up call. As we will
see, Rascals are rebels, but most importantly they are rebels *with
a cause*. This is what sets them apart from nihilists, egomaniacs,
brigands, and scoundrels. Rascals are different, to be sure, but they

are different for a purpose. They are different to make a difference. The effect of Rascals on others around them is important, as it leads to greater courage and loftier actions in an outward reaching ripple of influence. Rascals are the catalyst for positive actions, the fire starters of change, and the harbingers of advancement.

What is the alarm which requires a wake-up call? It is the chilling fact that individual freedom in our country and around the world is under attack. The principles and protections of individuals to live their own lives, make their own choices, and determine their own destinies are rapidly disappearing. Freedom has only ever been granted or preserved under the might of those who were too strong to be enslaved, too caring to let others suffer, and too smart for dangerous dogmas. It is a shame for people to be born free, then grow up and forget all about it. Rascals, in essence, adhere to the proclamation: "Born free and acting like it." Rascals are the great amplifiers of the principles that allow people to be free. Once studying the Rascal type, you may never look at the world the same again, nor the world at you! And that, dear reader, is my greatest wish. May this book help you become just a little crazy in a sacred sort of way. The world needs it.

Chris Brady
July 2010
Terontola, Italy

CHAPTER 1

The Type

What has been handed down to Americans as a priceless document of history was at the time an act of treason against the most powerful empire in the world. A group of fifty-six men had gathered at the behest of their respective colonies to form the Continental Congress. This body had been conducting an against-the-odds feud with minimal funds and almost no experience. As the conflict escalated, and a return to the tranquil days of the past was no longer a possibility, Congress decided it necessary to declare their independence in a document officially unifying the cause of liberty for the colonies from the tyranny of King George III. It was a statement that would officially categorize them as enemies of the state.

To understand the magnitude of the risk taken by these fifty-six men, it is necessary to understand who they were. They consisted of twenty-four lawyers, twelve doctors, eleven businessmen, nine farm-estate owners, and several statesmen and pastors. All but two had families of their own, and most were considered wealthy. Almost half were under forty years of age. Robert Morris was the most successful businessman in Philadelphia, John Hancock was one of the richest men in North America, and Richard Henry Lee was from one of Tidewater Virginia's richest and most powerful family dynasties. Benjamin Franklin was world famous. Dr. John Witherspoon was president of the College of New Jersey (later re-named Princeton). These men signed a document pledging: ". . . for the support of this Declaration, with a firm reliance on the protection of divine providence, we mutually pledge to each other our lives, our fortunes, and our scared honor." For them, it was no vain boast. They were well known, educated, propertied, influential, family men risking it all for the cause of liberty.

Although their cause would ultimately prevail, these men would pay dearly for their boldness. All were singled out for capture for treason. As a result, most would suffer the persecution of manhunts. Several had sons die in the war. Many lost most if not all of their property. Some were forever separated from their families. Nine died of wounds either from battle or imprisonment. Indeed, when these men pledged *their lives, fortunes, and sacred honor*, many were forced to sacrifice the first two. None, however, gave up the third. Each of the fifty-six signers of the Declaration of Independence held fast to his declaration, refusing to give up, turn back, turncoat, or surrender.

History provides few examples of a pack of Rascals such as these. They took a bold stand, hung tough, and initiated a movement for freedom that would birth the most incredible experiment in government yet known to man. They weren't perfect, and they didn't do everything right. But they did make a remarkable commitment at a critical moment in world history, summoning the courage and the character to see it through till the end. Their conduct after the signing speaks louder than even their words placed upon the document so gloriously sanctified with their signatures. In short, they sacrificed their own personal peace and affluence for a cause and purpose greater than themselves.

Rascals are known by what they do. Their unique character produces fruit different from that of the vast majority of people. They are unique, but not for the sake of uniqueness. They don't conform, but not for the sake of nonconformity. They are rebellious, but not for the sake of rebellion. They sometimes become famous and receive recognition, but not for the sake of fame or accolades. Rather, they seem to respond to the calling of an inner voice: one that stands for principle and justice. They commit to their beliefs. They may sacrifice their peace and affluence, their lives and fortunes, *but never their sacred honor.*

Plato wrote, "A hero is born among a hundred, a wise man is found among a thousand, but an accomplished one might not be found even among a hundred thousand men." Rascals as a species are best described by this "accomplished" man of Plato. They are extremely rare, because their courage and individuality is so uncommon. They have the courage to be authentic, the character to be a character, and the convictions to be an original.

This rarity wields a power all its own. Rascals embolden those around them and attract others who aspire to such heights of courage and character. In this way, change radiates outward. In the words of Margaret Mead, "Never underestimate the power of a small group of committed people to change the world. In fact, it is the only thing that ever has."

In the Broadway operetta of 1928 entitled *The New Moon*, underdog Robert Misson dreams of inspiring an uprising to throw off the tyranny of his French king. In words that would be recognized by Rascals throughout history, he chants:

> Give me some men
> Who are Stout-Hearted Men
> Who will fight for the right they adore
> Start me with ten
> Who are Stout-Hearted Men
> And I'll soon give you ten thousand more
> Shoulder to shoulder, and bolder and bolder
> They grow as they go to the fore…

Misson might not have known it, but he was calling for Rascals.

Finding *You* in a *They* World

Mark Twain was one of literature's greatest Rascals. He was extremely creative and brave as a writer while taking American literature to new heights. He pioneered a unique dialogue style that reflected how people in the fledgling United States, particularly those in the south and west, actually spoke. For such colloquialism he received both glowing admiration and scathing criticism. The criticism came because he hadn't followed the rules. He hadn't obtained the blessing of the powers-that-be in the east-coast publishing world before thrilling fans with his rough and realistic style. The eastern intellectuals, apparently assigning themselves the role of language guardians, banned Twain's book, *Huckleberry Finn,* because it was "the veriest trash, rough, course and inelegant; more suited to the slaves than to intelligent, respectable people."

In our day and age, it is hard to understand just what the fuss was all about. Slang words in print are no affront to our modern sensibilities. There is certainly nothing in his pages worthy of the outrage and censorship he experienced.* In fact, we see fit to call some of his works classics and make them mandatory reading in our schools.

The answer is simple. Mark Twain had broken the rules. He hadn't asked for permission to be himself. He didn't get approval to be creative. He just called it like he saw it, and he saw it clearly. As he himself said, he was a "prodigious noticer."

What Mark Twain had encountered was something familiar to us all: the *Council of They*. *They* are the thought police, the guardians of political correctness, the masters of conformity, the keepers

---

* The exception to this is the term Twain used to refer to African Americans; a colloquialism as common in his day as it is offensive in ours. While it didn't sound nearly as shocking in his times, Twain employed it liberally throughout his works (particularly in *The Adventures of Huckleberry Finn*) to emphasize the point of their mistreatment. Some mistakenly assume the use of this term was the source of criticism against Twain in his day, when it was actually his coarse dialogue and anti-east coast, anti-segregation politics that offended his contemporaries' sensibilities.

of the status quo. It is *They* who struggle always to keep life the way *They* say it should be, who fight change, who persecute creativity, and hurl criticism at anything that smacks of originality or authenticity. *They* try to say who is "in" and who is "out." *They* seem to have so much power that good, creative people leave their lives on the shelf rather than face their wrath. *They* will try to influence how you live, what you do, whom you should marry, and how you should raise your children. *They* want control, obedience, and blind acquiescence.

In life there is no shortage of people who will tell you what you are supposed to be and how you are supposed to act. It is as if everyone is in a big line heading nowhere. Everyone is expected to march in step to the beat of someone else's drummer, being a good little soldier and doing what the crowd expects. The only problem is, that herd of people following along in step aren't going anywhere, and as long as anyone listens to them, he or she won't go anywhere either. What Rascals do is *get out of line*. In fact, many Rascals have heard most of their lives that they are out of line in one way or another! Rascals don't fall for the lure of going along or becoming someone else just to please others. Rascals follow their convictions and confidently head in the direction of their destiny, mindful of their Creator and not of the crowd.

Non-conformity is not what we are talking about, but rather, authenticity. Non-conformity seeks to be different merely for the sake of being different. But different is not a value in and of itself. Being right, courageous, purposeful, and in line with God's will for our lives is what it is all about. If this happens to be different from the crowd (and it usually will) then so be it. But there is no fruit in chasing difference for the sake of non-conformity.

The first rule of becoming a Rascal is to slay the dragon of *They*. Rascals, quite frankly, don't care what *They* say. Rascals don't take their cue from the peanut gallery. Rascals are driven by their own sense of purpose and direction. Rascals hear their own music, write their own melodies, and dance their own dance. As the saying goes,

> "You wouldn't worry so much about what others thought of you if you knew how seldom they did."

> **"You wouldn't worry so much about what others thought of you if you knew how seldom they did."**

The important thing is to discover the real *You* in a *They* world. Who are you and what has God created you to do? Do you know who you are? More importantly, do you know *whose* you are? Arriving at the correct answers to these questions will be fundamental to how you live your life and the results of a life so lived.

"Giving" Happiness

Many people think life is about an individual's happiness. Even in the founding documents of the United States is the Enlightenment philosophy of the right to the "pursuit of happiness." Understanding true happiness and how it is obtained is a major part to living an authentic life of Rascalinity.

One of the biggest traps is the thought that happiness can be obtained by direct pursuit. The route chosen by most for this pursuit is the seeking of pleasure. We somehow think that by gaining enough pleasure we will be happy. But the pursuit of pleasure is a con job. It results in the endless spiral of the pursuit of *more*. This is because pleasure is not fulfilling. As each thrill is experienced, we automatically seek and desire a bigger thrill, a higher high. We become desensitized to the previous pleasure and go for stronger stimulation the next time. With this fundamental in mind it is easy to understand our modern epidemic of addictions. It seems there are addictions to almost anything and everything these days, from drugs and alcohol to sex and gambling. At the root of it all, however, is the same empty pursuit of pleasure and more pleasure.

We chase after what we are convinced will bring us happiness, only to discover that it only brings emptiness. So we chase harder and pursue even more stimulation, and soon we find ourselves sinking in a race to the bottom, an endless downward spiral of despair.

Others think that in peace and tranquility happiness can be found. But this is an empty chase, as well. For in the land of peace and tranquility lives the disease of boredom. Insignificance breeds restlessness. Idleness begets shallowness. Soon, we have lost our confidence, courage, and direction. While there is certainly nothing wrong with a vacation, down-time, or a little rest; peace and idleness are not only insufficient for producing true happiness, but counter-productive.

Happiness can never be obtained by direct pursuit. It is only the by-product of right living, of purposeful living, of living one's true destiny. After all, we are the happiest when our actions and behaviors are in line with the highest, best picture we hold of ourselves. This picture must always include a life of significance, courage, integrity, sacrifice, and service to others if it is to bring fulfillment. The selfish life is not worth living. It should be obvious that the only way to BE happy is to GIVE happy. Service to others and active love are where happiness is to be found. And ultimately, I have found that only a life lived for God through a personal relationship with His Son Jesus Christ can bring true fulfillment and joy. The direct pursuit of happiness through pleasures and stimulation will never work, and instead will backfire with despair and emptiness.

> **The selfish life is not worth living.**

Living on Purpose

Hundreds of books have been written on finding one's purpose, any number of which provide great exercises and thought-provoking questions. Here is a quick review of the genre: What makes you come alive? What activities bring you the most excitement, fulfillment, and sense of accomplishment? Additionally, it is helpful to ask, in which areas do you seem to demonstrate the most capability? For which things do you demonstrate a natural aptitude? What actions seem to bring the most compliments and praise from others? What were your natural affinities as a child?

Finding one's purpose, to me, has always been like an archeology project. We don't so much determine our purpose and direction in life as much as we *discover* it. Little clues present themselves. We gain a little insight into something that makes us feel great, something that we are actually good at doing, and we dust off a little bit more of the artifact. We ask ourselves questions and dust off a little more. We pray for God's guidance in our lives. Something happens to us in life and a bit more is exposed. Over time, we gain a clearer and clearer picture of who we are and what we were created to do.

Sam Adams was a Rascal. As a young man he witnessed the humiliation of his father by what he perceived to be the heartlessness of the English government. He would never forget it. As an adult he would be among the first to react to a new series of laws and regulations from England which he felt were demeaning and humiliating to the American colonies. A tireless rabble-rouser, Adams formed Sons of Liberty groups in opposition to the crown, sponsored clandestine meetings, encouraged protests to be posted at the Liberty Trees, and perhaps most importantly, recruited other influential men such as John Hancock and John Adams to the cause.

In effect, Sam Adams was the initiator of the American Revolution. In fact, at Concord Green, the "Shot heard around the world" was quite possibly aimed at him! Just what were the British redcoats doing in Lexington and Concord that morning? The answer is that they had two objectives. The first: get the arms and munitions from the arsenal at Concord, thereby depriving the unruly populace of armament. The second: capture Sam Adams and John Hancock and bring them in for treason!

Sam Adams bravely set himself up as the man in the crosshairs of the English king. He was bold, tireless, unflappable, and insufferable. The secret to his long campaign against the most powerful empire on earth was his *purpose*. He believed strongly in what he was doing, saw his calling very clearly, and had an over-riding sense of justice that inspired his actions.

Rascals are driven by purpose. They have a sense of their own destiny and a deep conviction that they were called to something great. They are not lulled to sleep like most by the comforts and pleasures of this world. Instead, they realize their privileges are not for their pleasure, but rather for their purpose.

A sense of purpose drives the greatest accomplishments in life. Realizing that we were built with specific talents and abilities and committing to utilize them in the endeavors for which we were created is a key aspect to the mindset of a Rascal. As John Calvin wrote, "All who are ignorant of the purpose for which they live are fools and madmen." Rascals know they were called to a purpose larger than themselves.

> **A sense of purpose drives the greatest accomplishments in life.**

Meaning It

A Rascal in touch with his purpose will never have trouble finding meaning in what he does. On the contrary, how many people fulfill Thoreau's lament of "leading lives of quiet desperation?" How many go to jobs they can't stand? How many people are just getting by, tip-toeing through life trying to get to death safely? How many are simply surviving when they could be thriving? How many are merely driving on their part of the roads, breathing their share of the air, eating their share of the food, and mindlessly passing through the days of their lives as though they will live forever?

Even the pagan Marcus Aurelius almost two thousand years ago said, "Do not live as though you have a thousand years."

> "Do not live as though you have a thousand years."
> - Marcus Aurelius

I like the moment in the movie *Braveheart* when William Wallace, in prison anticipating his execution, refuses to take a drug to deaden the pain. It is at that moment when he says, "Every man dies, not every man really lives."

Here is something that is very important to understand: You will make it financially. You will find a way to pay your bills and pass through financial pressure. You will be all right. Now don't get me wrong. I understand the power of financial problems and am not minimizing the real emotional burden that comes with them. I know how it feels to be crushed under the weight of not knowing where the next money is going to come from, wondering how the bills will be paid, and then having something else break and not having the funds to fix it! But it is this exact bondage to finances that keeps many, many people from really living. It is this pressure that keeps people from trying something new, from taking a risk, or from pursuing their life's dreams.

> "Our greatest fear should not be that we won't succeed, but that we will succeed at something that doesn't matter."
> - D. L. Moody

One of my all-time favorite quotes is from D. L. Moody: "Our greatest fear should not be that we won't succeed, but that we will succeed at something that doesn't matter." We can become so caught up in the process of surviving that we forget all about living. We behave as though the question of making it financially is somehow in doubt.

Granted, there have been many times throughout history and are even many places on this earth right now where merely surviving is an act of monumental heroism. There are wars, genocides, famine, and disasters. People who persevere through these horrors and somehow survive to live another day are heroes in their own right. But that is not the condition of most people reading this book in North America. Most people in the United States and Canada are nowhere near starvation, genocide, or war in their streets. Instead, we have been gifted peace and opportunity. We have been the recipients of the blood and sacrifice of others and have more liberty and freedom than almost anyone else in the world. The question is: what are we going to do with it? Are we going to worry about tight finances and get distracted by the minutia of getting by? Or are we going to have the boldness and character to go for accomplishment and significance? The reason I like that D. L. Moody quote so much is that it reminds us that we shouldn't be fearful of whether or not we will succeed, but that we should instead be fearful *we will waste our lives.*

Rascals do not waste their lives. Rascals do not live for meaningless purposes. Instead, Rascals are a breed apart. They strive for greatness and significance, knowing deep down that it matters how they live their lives and what they do with the time they've been given. If they have any fear at all, it is that they will not utilize their gifts and talents to the fullest. Rascals look to significance and contribution, striving to be worthy of the man referred to in the Phillips Brooks quote: "Be such a man, and live such a life, that if every man were such as you, and every life a life like yours, this earth would be God's paradise."

Courage as the Backbone

Having a healthy fear of wasting one's life is one thing, but allowing other fears to hold one back from pursuing a purposeful life is another. Rascals are not fearful by nature. They may feel fear, as everyone does, but it is how they respond to that fear that sets them apart. In essence, Rascals feel the fear and do it anyway!

Courage is not the absence of fear. It is action in spite of fear. As the saying goes, "Do the thing you fear and the fear goes away."

It seems there is a significant lack of courage in our culture today. Perhaps three generations of television and movies, two generations of video games, and the softening of a society at peace has taken its toll. Perhaps "we the people" have lost a bit of the grit demonstrated by our ancestors who shouldered the rifles, charged the beaches, immigrated on last hopes, and pioneered and planted. But it can be regained, one individual at a time; one *Rascal* at a time.

Author Gus Lee writes, "Courage is the single most decisive trait in a leader." I would add that it is the most decisive trait in a *Rascal*, as well, as Rascals, every last one of them as defined in this book, are leaders. Rascals are not seduced by avoidance, but are instead compelled to hit things head-on. When

> **Success and significance are *always* on the other side of inconvenience or fear.**

challenges or tough times arise, Rascals charge right in. Remember: success and significance are *always* on the other side of inconvenience or fear.

The Wright brothers were certainly Rascals. They even went against their father in pursuing their dream of mechanized and sustainable flight. Eventually their breakthrough moment awaited them. It was obvious that the next step in the development process of their apparatus was to gain actual experience controlling the flying surfaces. This could only be done by actively flying the machine themselves. This was extremely dangerous, but it was the only road between them and success. Wilbur Wright said of this fateful decision, "If you are looking for perfect safety, you will do well to sit on the fence and watch the birds; but if you really wish to learn, you must mount a machine and become acquainted with its tricks by actual trial." For someone like myself who has enjoyed motorized adventure his whole life, this quote is very inspiring! But it applies even more directly to a purposeful life well-lived. There is no safety in a significant life, and there is no sig-

> **There is no safety in a significant life, and there is no significance in a safe life.**

nificance in a safe life. It is a choice: a choice of courage.

Courage is one of the most important attributes in a true Rascal. In fact, one can't really become a Rascal without it. Again to quote Lee: "Courageous leadership is about utilizing all of our brains, character, and spirit to advocate principles regardless of the odds, heedless of fear, apart from collateral impact, and independent of personal career needs."

Rascals have the courage of their convictions and they act accordingly; mindless of fear, driven by purpose. As Eleanor Roosevelt said, "You gain strength, courage, and confidence by every experience in which you really stop to look fear in the face."

Danger, Danger

Risk is that action taken which puts something of value in danger for the sake of principle or gain. It should be obvious by this point that Rascals don't play it safe. They realize that the most dangerous move of all is playing for safety. In the words of Benjamin Franklin, "They who can give up essential liberty to obtain a little temporary safety, deserve neither liberty nor safety." Security and safety are natural human needs; there is nothing wrong with the desire for a little of both. But in a world rife with injustice and suffering, safety and security are not the highest values. Truth and justice, freedom, liberty, and the essential eternal questions are much more important. And any time someone sacrifices the

33

higher values for the sake of receiving more safety or security, he or she is lacking courage.

It is possible to tell what people value by watching what they will sacrifice to protect their safety and security. Most of the time when someone loses courage it is because something such as money, safety, comfort, or peace is held more dearly than the principle being challenged. Sometimes this involves danger to their physical self, but in our modern, civilized world, it is more likely a threat to peace and comfort. People will stand on principle as long as it doesn't cost them anything. They will shout platitudes from the rooftops as long as nobody messes with their pensions and benefits. It is when the prospect of the loss of ease or comfort becomes a stark reality that the courage of a Rascal reveals itself. It's when a person is willing to risk for the sake of a greater gain, or even more importantly for the sake of higher principles, that true mettle is displayed. There are millions who will say the right words, there are hundreds of thousands who will 'act' the part, but only a few, only the Rascals, will actually risk everything else for the sake of their principles.

Rascals understand risk and don't flinch in the face of it. They know that playing it safe is not safe at all. Instead, they take stock of their beliefs, hold firm to their principles, become informed about the dangers, and then act shrewdly but boldly.

And Justice for All

Harriet Tubman was born into slavery. Her young life embodied all the horrors of that era; abuse, separation from loved ones, whippings, and beatings. During one of the latter, she obtained a head injury that would plague her throughout her life.

Then things changed. In 1849 Tubman managed to escape. Incredibly, she quickly re-entered slave territory to help free her family. The dangers of doing so were enormous. Being recaptured would bring physical torture, and possibly death. Under the laws at the time, there was absolutely nothing to protect her. In fact, the laws were on the side of the slave-owners and the protection of their "property." Tubman, however, was driven. After successfully rescuing her own family, she returned again to help others. Utilizing the network of safe houses of sympathetic whites in the south and along the borders with the north, Tubman and others developed a system for freeing slaves that became known as the Underground Railroad. Tubman was especially capable at clandestine operations, moving mostly at night. She was so covert that most of the authorities had no idea it was Tubman they were seeking.

In 1850, United States law got even worse with the passage of the Fugitive Slave Act. This legislation was aimed at appeasing southerners by forcing those in free states to return escaped slaves back to their "owners." Effectively, the new law made it illegal to aid or harbor an escaped slave in any way, even in free states. Tubman and the Underground Railroad quickly adjusted, taking its "passengers" all the way to Canada for safety. In all, Tubman made somewhere between thirteen and nineteen trips into slave territory to free others. She would later say with pride, "I never lost a passenger."

When the Civil War erupted, Tubman volunteered as a nurse and cook. It wasn't long, however, before her covert abilities were put to use again. She was utilized as a scout, and at some points as a spy. Most incredibly, however, she became the first woman in the Civil War to lead an armed group. Her famous Combahee River Raid into the heart of South Carolina liberated somewhere between 750 and 1000 slaves. Tubman's "passenger" counts were getting bigger.

Following the war, Tubman established a home for aging former slaves, and became involved in the cause of women's rights. Health challenges eventually caught up with her, and her injuries from youth bothered her more and more. It was only at that point that the plucky Tubman was finally halted from fighting for the freedom of others. She had persisted through the fear of danger, the wrath of slave-hunters, and the guns of the Confederate army, literally wearing herself out in the name of liberty.

One of the most significant distinguishing characteristics of Rascals is their sense of justice. Rascals feel compelled to attack injustice wherever they find it. In fact, many throughout history were little more than faces in the crowd until confronted by something that offended their sense of right and wrong. William Wilberforce was a young man in the English Parliament when he was confronted by abolitionists who exposed him to the horrors of the slave trade. As a result, much to the detriment of his own political career, he spent the rest of his life pursuing its elimination. Irene Morgan, Sarah Louise Keys, Claudette Colvin, and Rosa Parks were just normal people living their lives when each became fed up with segregated bus seating in the south. All four decided enough was enough and, by refusing to give up their seats, made a stand that kicked off the Civil Rights movement in the United States.

There are many, many places in this world where injustice flourishes. All we have to do is care enough to look with eyes backed by a strong sense of right and wrong, paired with an empathy for those unfairly affected. Rascals everywhere share these traits. They stand firm in the face of wrong, fighting for what is right simply because it is right. G.K. Chesterton wrote, "Children are innocent and love justice, while most adults are wicked and prefer mercy." In a way, Rascals maintain a child-like sense of justice, uncorrupted by the callousness and cynicism that often develop with adulthood.

The Individualism of Originality

In the words of Ethan Embry, "You just have to do your own thing, no matter what anyone says. It's your life." Originality comes from the strength of character that allows us to "feel comfortable in our own skin." We can't truly succeed until we allow ourselves to be who we really are. A major part of this is understanding *whose* we are, realizing that we were created by an infinite God who loves us and has plans for us in His kingdom. True success, and the fulfillment that accompanies it, will not happen until we have the courage and character to become the original God intended. The world doesn't need any more copies; it desperately yearns for unique, authentic characters. As Howard Thurman said, "Don't ask what the world needs. Ask what makes you come alive, and go do it. Because what the world needs is people who come alive."

> The world doesn't need any more copies; it desperately yearns for unique, authentic characters.

There is no shortage of people in this world who will assign to us their expectations. They will attempt to impute onto us their perception of who we should be and how we should act. Some may even have our best interest at heart. But the biggest part of success in life is choosing our own path and answering that inner call that only we can hear. After all, it is *our* life. We alone are responsible for how we live it. Otherwise, we will be just like everyone else.

As Oscar Wilde wrote, "Most people are other people. Their thoughts are someone else's opinions, their lives a mimicry, their passions a quotation." This is never true of a Rascal. Rascals are individuals, and by being themselves, they are some of the most unique people anywhere. They do their own thing, and they do it their own way. As war correspondent John Dos Passos wrote, "Individuality is freedom lived."

> "Most people are other people. Their thoughts are someone else's opinions, their lives a mimicry, their passions a quotation."
> - Oscar Wilde

Rascals are unique originals in a world of copies. In the classic novel *The Brothers Karamazov*, Alyosha Karamazov gives some advice to a brilliant adolescent: "You are like everyone else, that is, like very many others. Only you must not be like everybody else, that's all. . . . Yes, even if every one is like that. You be the only one not like it. Don't be like every one else, even if you were the only one."

On Your Honor

It may seem counter-intuitive that we would describe a Rascal as being honorable. The more one understands the nature of a true Rascal, as defined in these pages, the more it should be obvious that *our kind* of Rascal is honorable above all things.

Honor is such a lost article in today's society that it almost sounds old fashioned. One definition of honor comes from Walter Lippman; "He has honor if he holds himself to an ideal of conduct though it is inconvenient, unprofitable, or dangerous to do so." But this doesn't go far enough, as it only posits "an ideal of conduct." Holding to one's values or ideals is certainly considered by some to be honorable, but *what of* those values? Didn't the Communists in Bolshevik Russia hold to their own values as they murdered millions of innocent people who refused to "enjoy the benefits" of socialism? No, holding to one's values even if costly is not the total picture. Thomas Jefferson's definition is much better: "Nobody can acquire honor by doing what is wrong." That says it. There is a right and a wrong, and honor is the result of adhering to what is right. Now, to add Lippman's part: *no matter what. That* is honor.

The United States Congressional Medal of Honor has only been awarded 843 times since the end of World War II. With behavior exemplary of the award, the example of Major General James E. Livingston is superb. It is perhaps a better rendition of honor than any definition. In a fierce battle in the village of Dai Do in Viet Nam, Livingston and his Marine unit fought to rescue another trapped Marine company that had been cut off from the others. Wounded twice by grenades, Livingston refused medical aid and continued fighting to successfully relieve the stranded company. Then a fresh marine battalion attacked the neighboring village of Dinh To and was heavily repulsed. Livingston garnered the remainder of his fighting force and volunteered to go to their aid as well. Wounded a third time and unable to walk or even get up, Livingston continued firing his weapon while pinned to the ground. In effect, Livingston and his men rescued not one but two fighting units from sure destruction that day. His comment upon the affair and his subsequent award speak to the spirit of honor adhered to by all Rascals:

> "When you are involved in an operation like this, you are doing everything for your buddies and for their welfare— you don't want to let your buddies down. I was responsible for the mission. I had to live with the results. A fellow Marine's life could depend upon my actions, and I would have to live the rest of my life with my decisions."

Taking responsibility and adhering to that responsibility even when things get tough, not wanting to let down those who depend upon you, and realizing you will have to live with the results of your decisions, are all demonstrative of what honor is all about.

Today, many people live by the rules of expediency instead. This means that, regardless of principles, if something works out to their benefit they do it; if not, they don't. It's like a newspaper that prints a juicy yet inaccurate article, then retracts it in a future publication. Truth is not that important because both the libel and its repeal were successful in selling papers. Unfortunately, this is too true of how the world works today. Pragmatism dominates. We have witnessed so many corporate, political, and Hollywood scandals that we are in danger of becoming jaded. Cynicism sets in as we feel like everyone is a crook, cheater, liar, and phony. Some people seem to think if everybody else appears to be "getting away with it" that maybe they can too. Gray areas become wide, pragmatism rules the day, and little white lies become the norm.

This downward spiral is even more reason to celebrate true Rascals like Major General Livingston. Most of us will never be asked or required to shoulder a rifle in the face of an enemy bent upon our destruction. But we will all be faced with foes, unfair situations, and troubling circumstances. Rascals live honorably through it all.

Learn to Discern

In the aftermath of World War II, Germany was, quite obviously, in shambles. This was not only true of its infrastructure, but of its economy, too. In 1948, after three years of governance under the Allied occupation, its economy was still no better off than it had been immediately following the war. The Allied authorities enforced price controls, wage fixing, rations, and centralized command control at all levels. It was Communism in everything but name. And, of course, it didn't work. Production was stymied, shelves were bare, and chaos reigned. The people were forced to barter like medieval peasants for basic goods and necessities. Alcohol, nylons, cigarettes, and chocolate became primitive forms of money. All this was happening in what had been one of the most sophisticated, intellectual, educated populations in the world.

Then in 1948, the economist Ludwig Erhard was elected Director of Economics for the Bizone; the area of Europe jointly occupied by both the United States and Great Britain. Erhard, who had been wounded as an artilleryman in World War I and therefore unable to fight in World War II, had instead spent his time planning for German peacetime recovery following the war. For this he had fallen from favor with the Nazis and lost his job. Now, however, he had his chance.

Erhard moved quickly. Entirely overstepping his authority, and going against the opinions of many officials from Germany and the occupying countries, he immediately abolished the price and wage controls and thereby opened Germany's economy to free market principles. He even went on public radio to announce his changes during a holiday in which most of the occupational authorities were absent. General Lucius Clay, the American military governor for Germany, sternly reproached Erhard. Clay bemoaned that all of his advisors were adamant that eliminating the economic controls would be a disaster. Erhard famously answered by saying, "Pay no attention to them, General, my advisors say the same thing."

Erhard's maneuver was daring and sweeping, demonstrating an enormous ability to discern good policy from a swirl of bad. It worked. Almost immediately the German economy began recovering. Incentive had been brought back into the lives of Germany's business people. Free market forces transferred accurate and timely information from millions of customers to millions of merchants and the entire supply chain aligned its supply to demand. The metrics of recovery were impressive. Six million new jobs were created in just a decade. Unemployment fell by a factor of ten. Overall economic growth averaged more than eight percent for over a decade. Germany recovered, and Erhard's policies were called the "Economic Miracle."

Stephen Covey wrote, "Wisdom is your perspective on life, your sense of balance, your understanding of how the various parts and principles apply and relate to each other. It embraces judgment, discernment, and comprehension," using the word *discernment* to help define wisdom. Discernment is the ability to comprehend what may be obscure. It is a rare quality, indeed; but accurate assessment of the events and situations around us is critical to proper decision making. Ef-

> **Discernment is the ability to comprehend what may be obscure.**

fective decision making, in turn, is fundamental to achievement.

Learning to decipher the complex messages of life's events, picking through the confusion and noise to find the key elements, is the hallmark of effectiveness. In the realm of dealing with people and circumstances, good discernment lies firmly in the category of *art,* meaning it is not easily learned from exposition and platitudes but must be acquired through living and critical thinking. This is nearly proven by its rareness. Discernment, understanding, and good judgment are uncommon because the act of thinking is so largely avoided by the masses. As Henry Ford once quipped, "Thinking is the hardest work there is, which is the probable reason why so few engage in it."

Discernment for Rascals means that they don't fall for the things that average, undiscerning people do. For instance, Rascals don't believe everything they hear on the news. They don't buy into everything they read on the Internet. And they certainly don't take as truth everything spoken by politicians. Rascals maintain a healthy dose of protective skepticism, insulating them against the failures of naiveté. Rascals agree with the statement, "In God we trust; all others must bring data." This is one of the essential contributions of Rascals in any society. Where the masses are led to the slaughter by tyrants who tickle their ears and promise them "bread and circuses," Rascals are awake and alert, standing in defiance. Dictators and socialists may fool most of the people all the time, but they will never fool the Rascals.

In the Bible, Proverbs 4:7 states "Wisdom is the principal thing: therefore get wisdom: and with all thy getting get understanding," indicating that an active pursuit of wisdom is of massive importance, and that coming to an accurate understanding of the world around us, though difficult, is paramount. Rascals pursue uncommon discernment and active understanding, but interestingly, nobody gets this one right all the time. That is when it is good to remember that bad decisions make for good stories!

André de Jongh

During World War II, Britain's valiant airmen were magnificent in their stand against the fierce German Luftwaffe. German bombers would cross the English channel intent on attacking civilian population centers and would be met with the plucky, hard-working, outlandishly brave pilots of the Royal Air Force (RAF).

As the fighting continued day after day it became increasingly difficult to find enough British airmen to keep in the sky. Many pilots flew for hours on end, coming back to land only long enough to refuel before taking off to fight again. Thousands of pilots were shot down over northwestern Europe, and it wasn't long before clandestine operations sprang into place to smuggle them back to England to fight again. Most of these 'escape lines' forming in Holland, Belgium, and France were established under the professional guidance of trained agents.

One of the most successful lines, however, was established and run by mere concerned citizens, the majority of them young and idealistic, dedicated to keeping the RAF fully stocked with pilots. This line would grow to become one of the most successful of all, accounting for over one fourth of the 2,900 airmen returned to Great Britain through escape lines between September 1939 and June 1944. Even more surprising, perhaps, was its driving force; a twenty-four year old woman named Andre de Jongh.

Jongh was raised in Belgium and familiar with the heroics of Edith Cavell, a woman executed in World War I for helping soldiers escape the Germans. Jongh had promised herself that if war ever came to her country, she would follow the example of Cavell. In May of 1940 Jongh got her chance when the

German armies marched into Belgium. At first Jongh did what she could by volunteering in an army hospital. It was here she noticed the strict observations of the German secret police. As more and more British soldiers came into the hospital, Jongh felt the increasing pull to do something about it. Without funds, experience, formal training, or permission of any kind, Jongh designed an escape route intent on outfoxing the Gestapo, what W. E. Armstrong called "the most efficient and cruelly repressive secret police in Europe." It would necessitate the involvement of hundreds of clandestine volunteers risking their lives to transport escapees across three national borders, all the way south through Europe, across the Pyrenees, and finally to Gibraltar. From there the airmen would be returned by ship to Britain to fight again.

Jongh began smuggling escapees along her route, enlisting the support of the British consulate in Bilbao, upon whom she left a very favorable impression. Jongh demanded autonomy and permitted no interference in her operations, negotiated shrewdly, and soon received funding and contacts for support. Journey after arduous journey proved successful, and soon, Jongh was in trouble. The Brussels Gestapo had detected her involvement and slated her for arrest. Her father got word to her during one of her escape runs that she could not return to Belgium. He calmly took over in her place as she continued to run the line remotely.

Airmen safely delivered back to Britain soon began singing the praises of the youthful and vigorous André de Jongh. They were in near disbelief that such a fragile and warm-hearted figure should be so brave in the face of mortal risk. The legend of André de Jongh grew and grew. Accordingly, the Gestapo predictably increased their efforts to find her and eliminate her escape line, which now was being called The Comet Line by the British secret service, after the behavior of comets in the sky to disappear and reappear again without warning. They arrested and tortured over one hundred of the line's volunteers; but nobody cracked under pressure, and Jongh was still safely at large. Then, during her thirty-third passage, Jongh was finally arrested. Moved from prison to prison, the attempts of her own Comet line to rescue her all failed. Finally, she was moved to concentration camps. Throughout this time she was brutally interrogated twenty-one times, revealing nothing more than the fact that she was the master behind the Comet Line; a fact doubted by the Gestapo.

Incredibly, the Comet Line lived on. Inspired by Jongh's example and empowered by her organization, new volunteers seemed always ready to step into gaps created by arrests and murders. Young person after young person was on hand to assume the responsibility of leadership at each of the key steps along the escape line. "We felt we couldn't let her down," said Elvire de Greef, another young woman, "Dedee [De Jongh] was not simply the founder of Comet, she *was* Comet."

Although Jongh's father and hundreds of others were arrested and/or shot, eventually the Allied armies liberated Europe and André de Jongh herself was freed. One pilot said, "André de Jongh was one of those rare beings who felt the misery of the world and would not let it rest." There could be no better description of a true Rascal!

CHAPTER 2

The Strengths

I Have a Dream

Dario Brose was only four years old when he saw his father collapse with a heart attack while playing soccer. A few years later his mother and her two little boys moved to Germany to be near family. While there, little Dario witnessed his first top-level professional soccer match. "It was incredible," says Brose, "once I saw that first game I *knew* I wanted to be a professional player. Soccer became absolutely everything to me!" Eventually the Brose's would move back to the United States, but Brose's dream drove him to take a bold step. At age thirteen he returned alone to Germany to try out with one of Germany's top professional team academies. "I needed to go back, and somehow I convinced my mom to let me. But when I got over there it was tough, very tough. Nobody talked to me at all, even the coaches. I would hear shuffling around in the hallway and guessed it was time to assemble for training or whatever. Nobody told me anything. The training was very physically demanding, but that wasn't the worst of it. The mental aspect was by far the toughest. Nobody talked to me, the kids were very against having an American over there, I guess, and the atmosphere was so serious and stern I could hardly believe it. Everybody seemed angry. These kids were serious about becoming professional players; all of them." Brose never even got the chance to play in any of the scrimmage games. At the end of the training, he was dropped off at the wrong train station and left to fend for himself. "I just chalked it up as a learning experience," he said.

Brose didn't quit, however. He still had the burning desire to become a professional player. But he had another obstacle: no matter where he went or how well he played, he was always the smallest player. "I decided not to let that stop me. Instead, I would figure out what to work on to come back better and stronger the next week. I don't know if it was pride or whatever that drove me, I was just so determined." So determined, in fact, at age seventeen Brose decided to head back to Germany to give it another try. This time he bought a one-way ticket.

Again with a top-level team, knowing a little more what to expect, Brose was still ridiculed and attacked. This time the kids fouled and tackled him incessantly in an effort to take him out. While on the ground, they would say to him in German, "It's part of the game." Brose says, "I got so beat up and discouraged that I called my brother on the phone and cried. 'I don't know if I can do this. They are killing me.' Then my brother asked me, 'Have you at least shown them what you can do? Why don't you go out there and kill someone first, don't pass the ball, give it your all, then come home after that if you're going to come home.' So that's what I did. I tackled this one kid with a totally vicious tackle and said to him in German, 'It's part of the game.' After that game, the coach said he wanted me to stay. In the first youth game they played me in, people came out to watch the American play, but nobody on the team would pass me the ball. I asked the coach about it and he said, 'just play.' Finally, I got my chance and scored with a bicycle kick . . . the crowd went nuts. From that day on, they knew I could play. I couldn't have scripted it better!"

Ultimately, Brose played as a professional in France for three years, Germany for four, and the United States for three. With the United States men's team, Brose played in the 1992 Barcelona Olympics, despite one U.S. national team coach telling him, "You are too small." Brose may have been small, but his dream was big.

We have already discussed purpose and meaning at great length. But the topic is so paramount to a Rascal's success that we must analyze it at a different angle to fully understand the power toward accomplishment contained in a dream. In fact, given two Rascals with equal ability and opportunity, the one with the biggest dream will win every time.

Carl Sandburg said, "Nothing happens without first a dream," and this is true, but first it is necessary to distinguish between a dream and a fantasy. A dream is an over-riding,

> **"Nothing happens without first a dream,"**
> **- Carl Sandburg**

deep, burning desire given of God and requiring one's abilities to complete. A fantasy can look just like a dream, but it has no power to inspire action. The best way to know if something is a true dream is to see if it compels one to action. There are plenty of people who will say, "I want this" or "wouldn't it be nice to have that?" but a big dream is not a *nice to have* thing, rather, it's a *have to have* thing!

In our book *Launching a Leadership Revolution*, Orrin Woodward and I described the Three Levels of Motivation. The first level involves material success. This would include physical comforts, the trappings of success, toys and things, as well as charitable giving and money to take care of family and loved ones. The second level involves recognition and respect. This includes public awards, titles, honors, and the acknowledgement of mentors, peers, teammates, and even critics. The third level involves purpose, destiny, and leaving a legacy.

Each of these three levels contains the ability to inspire. Each holds many forms of dreams. In fact, it is recommended that people find dreams at each of the three levels. This is because different challenges require different levels of commitment. Sometimes a material dream will be sufficient to inspire performance. Other circumstances might require something deeper, something more along the line of respect or recognition or proving the critics wrong. Still other instances require something as deep and compelling as possible: a life's purpose, a cause much greater than oneself, a desire to leave a lasting and meaningful legacy.

Dreams must be strong for accomplishments to be mighty. Dreams should be sufficient to empower a Rascal to perform, overcome his or her fears over a long period of time, drive toward excellence, and avoid the many snares, distractions, and temptations that lurk in ambush for all achievers.

> **Dreams must be strong for accomplishments to be mighty.**

Strong dreams are fundamentally important in the life of achievement, though most people don't realize it. The tendency is to see someone at a certain station in life and think that he or she was always at that level of success, or somehow lucky. Nothing could be further from the truth. The Walt Disney theme parks that are so much a part of the world's culture today sprang from the mind and dreams of one man, and took years and years to come to fruition. Steven Spielberg, one of Hollywood's most famous moviemakers, was sneaking onto the production lot of Universal Studios as a young teen, constantly dreaming of the day he himself would make movies. Jon Bon Jovi, one of the world's most successful musical recording artists and performers, said that from the time he was a child all he wanted to be was a rock star. Sylvester Stallone was nearly homeless and needed money so badly he even had to sell his dog during the years he was marketing his script for the movie *Rocky*. Each of these individuals were driven by a dream so strong in their hearts that it propelled them through hardship, challenges, and all manner of obstacles standing in their way. There was nothing automatic about their success; rather, it was the direct result of the strength of their respective dreams.

An Out of Sight Vision

One of the biggest psychoses of modern living is the expectation of quick success. In a micro-wave society, people have come to expect things *now*. They complain when their fast food requires more than a minute or two of preparation or when a trans-continental flight is delayed for thirty minutes. Of course, however, *Roma non fu fatta in un giorno*: Rome was not built in a day. True success requires time, patience, and a long term view.

Having long term vision is not as easy as one might think. As we have discussed, it first requires a strong, big dream. If the dream is the motivation, the vision is the projection of that dream on the canvass of one's future life. It is the focus of the view provided by the dream.

> **If the dream is the motivation, the vision is the projection of that dream on the canvass of one's future life.**

There are two parts to having a long term vision. The first part is the *term*. The longer the term of the vision, in most cases the more likely it is to come true. This is because people tend to overestimate what they can accomplish in one year and underestimate what they can in ten. It goes back to the concept of incremental improvement over time. If a dreamer is striving toward a vision, working hard toward mastery and improvement, time becomes an ally. But if the term is unrealistic by being too short, the dreamer gets disenchanted and loses belief.

The second part of a long term vision is the vision itself. The more detailed and real the vision, the more power it has to inspire. As the saying goes, "We don't always get what we want; we tend to get what we consistently *picture*." It stands to reason then that we want to make that picture in our mind's eye as clear as possible. Also, we want to go through the exercise of picturing it as often as we can. The more time we can invest visualizing our future success

51

scenarios, the more our actions will automatically gravitate in that direction. Decisions become easier and easier as our minds process them in the context of the future vision. If it fits, we'll do it. If it doesn't fit, we throw it out. Simple. In fact, life appears simple and straightforward to those with clear visions of their future. It is people without dreams and the corresponding long term views of their fulfillment that seem to squander their days and scramble around in wasteful energy.

The founding fathers of the United States were perhaps some of the most visionary statesmen of all time. With an eye firmly fixed upon the future they crafted America's founding documents with admirable prescience. They carefully established a Constitution that has mostly withstood the test of time. The corresponding Bill of Rights has served as a fence of protection against the encroachment on individual freedoms of a growing government. What they created with incredible long term vision was a government that has outlasted all others on the face of the earth. Every other country has formed or re-formed its government since the days of America's founding.

The vision of the founders was so acute, in fact, it was able to foresee where potential demise might occur. All one need do to discover proof of this is read the *Anti-Federalist* papers. As early as the culmination of the drafting of the Constitution, Benjamin Franklin gave a prophetic warning. To a woman passing by the Pennsylvania State House who inquired, "Well, doctor, what sort of government have we?" Franklin replied, "A republic, if you can keep it." As time has now shown, the greater vestiges of the republican government as created in the Constitution are what have suffered the most damage over two and a quarter centuries. Franklin's prediction is astounding. These were men with extraordinary long term vision. They beheld a great country in their minds' eyes and struggled mightily to create it from a small, agrarian community. And they even saw the fault lines along which it might crumble.

Illumination of Inspiration

Inspiration can be considered the impulse of conviction at a key moment; representative of what one truly is in all the other moments. Inspiration may come to us as a new insight, a flash of genius, or a moment of high motivation toward a goal. Poets and artists have referred to it as a "muse" who lights upon their shoulder from time to fleeting time, unleashing spurts of creative energy. Some have described the concept as a rush of creative energy; such as can keep a composer scribbling away for hours on end without eating or sleeping. Inspiration and the key moments it brings about are precious and can lead to massive results.

Often inspiration occurs at the point of confrontation with a problem. That is what happened with General Motors Vice President, Terry Woychowski, whose family had gotten involved in the sponsorship of an African outreach in Malawi, through the efforts of their church and the World Vision organization. The Woychowskis sponsored a ten year old boy named Solomoni Mufata. Solomoni, one of five children living with a single mother in an AIDs ravaged territory, began receiving financial support from the Woychowski family. But soon, he would receive much more.

As Terry Woychowski explains, "I often pray for him, and want to help instill in him a Godly way of life. I also want to help Solomoni lead a battle against corruption in his country and help lead his people to a better way of life. Then I received a background report on Solomoni which included his report card. He was failing all grades and was going to be required to repeat the second grade. I found this shocking and unacceptable." Woychowski decided to do something to help. He began by researching the reasons why Solomoni was doing so poorly in school; the biggest of which turned out to be truancy. Solomoni was missing a lot of school. Among other reasons, Solomoni is needed to help with the family chores, particularly the efforts involving the processing of corn, his family's staple food crop. This not only involves growing and harvesting the corn, but transporting it to another village and having it ground into a fine flour, a key ingredient in their main food. The grinding is done on a diesel powered hammer mill, which is fraught with problems and is not always reliable. Additionally, the whole process is expensive (estimated to consume about 30% of a family's annual income). Beyond the $15.00 per gallon fuel price, the grinder is a day's walk away from Solomoni's village. This means that young Solomoni must carry a 40 pound bag of corn on a day's march, spend money and another day getting it ground, then carry it back home again on the third day. No wonder little Solomoni's education was slipping when it took so much to simply survive. Worst of all, however, was the fact that Solomoni's situation was not unique but typical for his region of the world.

Woychowski, a leadership guru and serial engineer, knew just what to do. He marched into a regularly scheduled meeting in which he mentors a select group of up-and-coming automotive engineers (who have named themselves "Terry's ARMY" after the characters in the Harry Potter series who styled themselves as "Dumbledore's ARMY"), gave a short presentation about Solomoni and his dilemma, and said simply, "Fix this. Use the best fifty minutes to create a plan that the ARMY can implement to address the failing performance of Solomoni." One can only imagine the looks on the faces of the young protégés as they wondered if their mentor was serious. Quickly the group got to work and dug up information and crafted action plans. One of these plans led to a Senior Design Project at Michigan Technological University to design and develop a human-powered hammer mill, built from inexpensive component parts readily attainable in the local African villages. Sponsorship would be provided by the Woychowski Charitable Foundation, and development would take place at Michigan Tech. Next, The World Hope organization agreed to build and test several units, pending a viable design.

The result was the first ever workable human-powered hammer mill. World Hope has now begun installing mills in Zambia to test performance. David Erickson of World Hope reported that the mills "are generating a lot of excitement." The human-powered hammer mills have the potential to ease the burden of thousands of sub-Saharan families and may also help small businesses prosper because of lower corn processing costs. If successfully implemented, the ramifications of the hammer-mill project would be truly immeasurable.

That's how it works with inspiration in the life of a Rascal. Caring enough to dig into a problem thousands of miles away caused a pivotal moment of inspiration for Terry Woychowski and his ARMY of young protégés. They spotted a challenge and decided to do something about it. The ideas flowed as a result. What began as a way to help a ten year-old boy turned into something far larger, spanning several organizations and continents and loaded with the potential to affect thousands. That's the power of inspiration in the hands of leaders who care.

A Lean and Hungry Look

In the famous Shakespeare play *Julius Caesar*, Act 1, Scene 2, the following exchange occurs:

Caesar: "Antonio!"

Marcus Antonius: "Caesar?"

Caesar: "Let me have men about me that are fat,
    Sleek-headed men and such as sleep a-nights.
    Yond Cassius has a lean and hungry look,
    He thinks too much; such men are dangerous."

Caesar was correct. Cassius would be at the center of the successful plot to assassinate Caesar in the senate chamber. It was the *lean and hungry look* that tipped off Caesar, a consummate judge of character, to the ambition lurking beneath the surface in "Yond Cassius."

Again, we must be careful with our examples. I am most certainly not saying that a Rascal is someone who plots murder or stabs world leaders in senate chambers. However, it is instructive how keen Caesar was to the attributes that stood Cassius out from the crowd. It was Cassius's *lean and hungry look.* Historians have long argued whether Cassius' hunger stemmed from unbounded ambition or a more noble patriotism for the fast-disappearing Roman Republic. In either case, his hunger was obvious, at least to Shakespeare's character. Based of course on proper, clean motives, this is how Rascals should be when it comes to learning and being teachable. They should be lean and hungry for wisdom and learning. There should be something about them that differentiates them from the crowd, something "to make tyrants wonder." After all, Rascals are dangerous to the status quo.

> **Rascals are dangerous to the status quo.**

Learning can be one of the most enjoyable and rewarding experiences in life. For many this is a little hard to believe. Who among us hasn't had nightmare memories of final exams and pop quizzes? But we're not necessarily referring to formalized education, although that may play its part. Real learning is a lifelong process; in fact, it should be a lifelong *love.*

How is it that one falls in love with learning? The answer can be given in one word: relevance. Often complaints about formalized instruction stems from the root problem that we fail to see the relevance to our life. Maybe we ask, "When am I ever going to actually *need* this?" Therefore the best and most effective teachers know that all teaching must include the imparting of proper context and perspective. People will only pay attention to what interests them. Context and perspective allow the learner to understand how the subject matter fits his life.

Rascals don't wait for outside forces to provide this context, however, they go after it themselves. Realizing that they don't know what they don't know, Rascals dig in by learning all they can. This begins a process winners down through the ages have all utilized: self-directed education. A self-directed education is the hallmark of greatness. Many people incorrectly think that once through with their formal schooling they are done learning, as if to say: "Okay, that's it. Now I'm ready for life." But without personal growth driven from within, greatness cannot be achieved. In short, if you're through learning, you're through. From Julius Caesar and Hannibal to George Washington, Napoleon, Churchill and Lincoln, reading and self-learning have been critical components in development and achievement.

So once one realizes he must continue learning throughout life, he becomes more teachable as a result. Teach-ability represents an openness and eagerness of mind. A mind is like a parachute: it won't work unless opened. One of the reasons continuous learning is so important is that achievers can learn from those who have gone before them. Adopting the successful strategies and techniques of others is

> **A mind is like a parachute: it won't work unless opened.**

an effective shortcut on the route to success. More importantly, though, is the inculcating of correct *principles*. Methods are many, principles are few, methods always change but principles never do. A lot of pain and hardship can be avoided or more properly handled once we know the foundational principles of life. Success, also, comes about by operating in alignment with correct principles. Not knowing and living by these principles is the height of folly.

Rascals, then, put and keep themselves on a journey of lifetime learning. It is one of their biggest, most resilient weapons. They read good books, listen to audio recordings, attend events where they can associate with great teachers, and learn from others who are more advanced along the relevant success pathway. While others are drowning themselves in a deluge of entertainment and electronic fixation, Rascals are studying and preparing.

Devoted to Commitment

A great look into the commitment of a Rascal comes from Olehile Fischer Thataone who wrote, "We should remain true to our course; which may mean committing yourselves to things of which people around you would normally disapprove." Rascals sometimes commit to things and purposes the masses can't or won't understand. That's okay: it is the ability of a Rascal to commit to a worthy endeavor, no matter what others think, that separates him from the rest.

> It is the ability of a Rascal to commit to a worthy endeavor, no matter what others think, that separates him from the rest.

Nicolaus Copernicus was a star at his university in Krakow, Poland. Professors would display his mathematical abilities to outsiders with great pride. One of these visitors invited Copernicus to teach mathematics in Italy. It was there he heard his first lecture on astronomy. Immediately, Copernicus was smitten by the thought that mathematics could explain the movement of the stars.

For nearly a millennium and a half, most learned men clung to the descriptions of the heavens given by Ptolemy in his master work, *The Almagest*. It posited that the stars and sun revolved around the earth, which itself was the center of the universe. Additionally, most people down through the ages believed the earth to be flat. But as Copernicus made his own observations and discussed them with astronomers, he came to the realization that most of them had no workable understanding of mathematics. He realized the two fields should be used together to develop an actual system to describe God's wonder displayed each night in the heavens. Copernicus spent long night-time hours making observations and doing calculations. He came to agree with the radical notion that the earth was not at the center of the universe, but rather that it was a revolving body itself, orbiting the sun. He began sharing his mathematical proofs in his lectures, even using Columbus's recent voyage of discovery to the New World to debunk the myth of a flat world.

Then the trouble began. Priests and Cardinals began bashing him publicly for his work. In their view he was denouncing God, and they just couldn't handle the blow to their pride of believing that "the earth wobbles around the sun, like a moth around a lamp!" They were at the center of the universe and any contrary opinion was unacceptable. Copernicus countered that he was simply trying to accurately describe God's handiwork, and that nothing in his findings conflicted with scripture in any way. But the die was cast and Copernicus was forbidden to speak publicly on the subject at all. He returned to Poland in what can only be called a voluntary exile.

During his tenure as a humble canon in the cathedral in Frauenburg, Copernicus was watched closely by the religious and academic authorities. He fulfilled his duties as a clergyman faithfully, but all the while studied the stars, performed his calculations, and recorded what he was learning. He remained convinced of his conclusions, and was frustrated at his inability to publish them or discuss them openly. He took the greatest advantage of his situation, however, writing; "God has set me apart that I may study and make plain His works."

Copernicus had grown old and feeble, worn out by his long

struggles with authority and the permanent muzzle placed upon him. After forty years of toil, he had finally completed *On the Revolutions*, his master work that explained and proved his dangerous observations. Taking an enormous risk, but firmly committed to telling the truth, Copernicus had some friends secretly publish his book. There was a very real fear that the authorities would find out about it and destroy the original manuscript and notes before it could be duplicated for the world to read. Also, Copernicus was sick and dying and was afraid his great knowledge would die with him. The book, however, was successfully published in 1543, and as legend would have it, a first copy from production was placed into the hands of the infirm Copernicus mere moments before he died. He had remained faithful to his convictions all the way to the end. He had shown a commitment to the truth that would advance science for all of mankind in an enormous leap.

Truly committing to something and merely taking a stab at it are at opposite ends of the spectrum. As Art Turock wrote, "There's a difference between interest and commitment. When you're interested in doing something, you do it only when circumstances permit. When you're committed to something, you accept no excuses, only results." An illustration of this is the comparison between the chicken and the pig. For the purpose of providing breakfast the chicken may contribute, but the pig will have to be committed! That's the difference between commitment and anything else.

The Locus of Focus

These are busy times in which we live. Electronic media and technology have invaded nearly every aspect of our lives in the name of convenience. Many couples are each working jobs. Then there are the children, activities at church, chores around the house, banking and errands and obligatory parties and gatherings. Who among us hasn't felt the pressure of the hustle and bustle of our modern way of living?

It seems as if "busyness" has infected us all. None of us is immune. It calls to mind the quote from Henry David Thoreau who wrote, "It is not enough to be busy, so too are the ants. The question is, what are we busy about?" I have always liked this quote, because it cuts directly to the heart of the matter. Author Marshall Goldsmith states, "It is time to stop dreaming of a time when you won't be busy."

> "It is not enough to be busy, so too are the ants. The question is, what are we busy about?"
> - Henry David Thoreau

Apparently, being busy is just part of life. It has probably always been that way since the days when gathering fire wood, hunting, and preparing meals consumed all of one's time. But busyness is no excuse for lack of performance, or more importantly, lack of living an authentic, purposeful, significant life. We simply must find a way to cut through it all and make our days count.

Who hasn't tried some sort of time management tool? Who hasn't struggled to live according to one's priorities? It all makes so much sense when we sit through the lecture series or read the brochures, but when it comes to truly living these principles, things seem to go awry.

Rascals, however, find a way. They understand their priorities and find a way to align their actions accordingly. There are several factors that play into this. As we have already discussed, one way is to have a clear and definite purpose in mind. In the Bible we are told of three wise men traveling from the east around the time of the birth of Jesus. It is thought by historians that these men were likely from the land of Persia. A quick glance at the map shows many geographic obstacles between the heart of Persia and tiny Judea. We are told that these men traveled across these difficult and hazardous lands by following a bright star shining in the sky. This star provided a point of navigation to keep them on track no matter what challenges they encountered below; be it bandits, rivers, mountains, deserts, or jealous kings. In similar fashion, Rascals navigate through the pressures of their lives by progressing toward something solid and clear on their horizon. No matter what is encountered, a true Rascal can follow his own path if guided by a star in his future sky. Looking up is the best way to pass through things that can bring you down. It's when your focus is bigger than your obstacles that you can make progress.

> **Looking up is the best way to pass through things that can bring you down.**

Having clear and energizing goals is another major tactic to avoid the trap of busyness. Goals should be exciting, stretching, and specific. If they don't exert a power to perform, then they are not believable enough, not specific enough, or not short-term enough.

Goals make prioritization easy. One can simply ask, "Will this help me get closer to my goal?" If not, it shouldn't be done. Notice how difficult this becomes if there is no goal. But with a goal, one can look at anything and everything that comes along and determine, "Does this fit?" and "What's important next?"

This is all critical because the enemy of great is "*good.*" There are literally millions of *good* things out there we could be doing with our time. There are pass-times and hobbies and people and places to visit, things to explore and activities with which to become involved. Any of these things may be fine on their own. However, if we do not learn to distinguish between *great* and *good*, we will waste countless hours doing *good* things while missing out on the *great*. Focus is so important, and if we have a clearly defined goal, making decisions about what is *good* and what is *great* to do next becomes easier in light of that goal.

There is another concept that we will call 'pruning.' This is something a Rascal does every time he feels the press of too many things or activities around him. Somehow he has allowed too many commitments, interests, or distractions into his life. The only prudent thing to do at this point is to make adjustments, deciding that some things simply have to go. Which activities are not central to achieving the goal? Which are not directly in line with life's purpose? Which can wait until later? As hard as it may be, one has to get good at saying 'no' to a lot of *good* things in order to preserve space for the *great* things. In other words, a Rascal is slow to allow anyone to complicate his life.

It should be clear at this point that Rascals who achieve the most are the best at focusing upon what is most important in terms of their goals and overall purpose. They keep themselves free of the distractions of lesser things and ensure that their busyness is about something meaningful and in line with their larger purpose.

A Matter of Habit

The ancient poet Ovid wrote, "Nothing is stronger than habit." To a large degree, the habits we form will determine the results we achieve.

As humans we are habit-forming creatures. We get into grooves we hardly notice and just do things *the way we do them* over and over again. These things become second nature to us. For instance, most families don't hold a conference to determine which chairs at the kitchen table will be used by whom. Yet, over time, a habitual pattern develops in which each family member has his or her specific seat. It is the same with most things. We tend to shop at the same grocery store, making our way through the aisles in the similar pattern each time. We eat at the same few restaurants, even choosing the same table or booth repeatedly. We put on a certain shoe before the other, etc. These are just a glance at some of the habits representing thousands we develop over the course of living our lives.

What about the more important aspects to life? Habits are critical here, too. For instance, if we develop the habits of poor eating, alcohol intake, smoking, gossip, lying, cheating, sleeping too much, avoiding regular exercise, and any other such thing, we will sow the seeds of problems later on. This may result in broken health, relationships, finances, careers, and households.

The future condition of our lives in all categories lies hidden within the structure of our daily habits. This is because habits work both ways. We have considered many negative habits so far, but what about positive ones? What about eating healthy, exercising regularly, being honest, staying away from addictive substances and activities, and associating with honorable people? These are likewise habits which can be expected to produce results, although positive. Just as a watermelon seed grows watermelons, so too do the seeds of our habits generate the corresponding fruit.

> The future condition of our lives in all categories lies hidden within the structure of our daily habits.

Jim Ruyn says, "Motivation is what gets you started. Habit is what keeps you going." When it comes to achieving success and significance, our habits take over after the initial motivation flags. This is critical to understand. Knowing this, we can use our initial motivation for something to spur us into the development of a positive habit. Then, even if our motivation withers a bit under the pressure of life or the discouragement that guards all great accomplishment, we will already be in a productive habit. "But I don't *feel* like doing it," non-Rascals might say. The good news is you don't have to *feel* like it: you simply have to *do* it! Easier said than done? Maybe. But properly constructed habits are powerful. Once we get into the groove of doing something on a regular basis the habit mechanism takes over and makes it seem natural to us.

The Adroitness of Mastery

Rascals are able to boldly march in their own direction because of the confidence derived from their competence. Getting good at something is a great way to gain assuredness of direction. The better one gets at something the harder it is for anyone or anything to knock one off that path. Stated more simply, the harder you work at something, the harder it is to quit it.

Mastery is a concept little understood in today's world. We tend to glorify top-level athletes as "gifted," top business pioneers as "geniuses," and top leaders in many fields as "born" leaders. While there may be some truth to this, there is a lot of research to suggest that success is more about mastery than it is about inborn ability. Malcolm Gladwell wrote, "The question is this: is there such a thing as innate talent? The closer psychologists look at the careers of the gifted, the smaller the role innate talent seems to play and the bigger the role preparation seems to play."

This is why it is so important to understand the principles from the previous section about busyness; because anyone suffering from the effects of busyness will never be able to muster the focus required to obtain mastery of a certain subject. This is because mastery is the product of applied and focused practice over time. No focus, no mastery.

Most people do not understand the power of incremental improvements over time. The compounding effect of effort over the long haul is staggering to behold. The fact is that success requires mastery in one's chosen field. Mastery utilizes the compounding effect of effort over time. And there is a certain type of effort that is required: passionate and perfect.

Passionate effort is the kind that has heart behind it. There is a drive and a desire for success that empowers the development process. Half-hearted effort and practice is useless. If one is not passionate about what he is doing, some other area of endeavor should be chosen. As the mountain bikers say, "Go big or go home." Life is too short to fumble along in the wrong vocation. Rascals find something they can be passionate about, then pour their whole self into its mastery. They show up to practice early, work hard, demonstrate a desire to learn with a positive attitude, and push on through the pain of getting better.

Perfect practice is the other component, as it is the only kind of practice that leads to improvement. Anything else is wasted time at best, counter-productive at worst. Practicing for the sake of practicing, or simply to "put in the time" is not really practice, it is dishonesty. No one is served by a partial commit-

No one is served by a partial commitment.

ment. Also, practice that doesn't lead one to mastery of the fundamentals and to a mastery of proven techniques is also wasted time, because it leads to the learning of bad habits and ineffective methods. This is why the quality of coaching or mentorship is so important. A student on the journey toward mastery needs expert guidance and proper fundamentals.

The concept of mastery should be stimulating. This is because the message is that *anyone* can become great if he is willing to put in the time and effort over the long haul to fulfill his calling. Sure, there may be those who are bigger than you, faster than you, smarter than you, or better positioned within society than you. The facts are, however, that it doesn't matter. Victory goes to the one who decides to accomplish his dreams, then sets out consistently to master his craft, working hard over the long haul without faltering. What this all means is that achievement comes about as a result of commitment, and commitment is a choice. You can literally choose to become great because you can choose to master your craft.

No Shame in Hard Work

That choice, however, must be backed by hard work. Mastery only comes through hard work. The reason most people don't recognize opportunity is because it normally shows up dressed in work clothes. What happens to many is they find out that their dreams aren't really dreams but fantasies. They say, even to themselves, that they want to ac-

> **The reason most people don't recognize opportunity is because it normally shows up dressed in work clothes.**

complish this or that, but when the chance to move in that direction presents itself, they make excuses or procrastinate, avoiding the effort that follows commitment.

According to Gladwell, "The thing that distinguishes one performer from another is how hard he or she works. That's it. And what's more, the people at the very top don't work just harder or even much harder than everyone else. They work much, *much* harder. The idea that excellence at performing a complex task requires a critical minimum level of practice surfaces again and again in studies of expertise. In fact, researchers have settled on what they believe is the magic number for true expertise: ten thousand hours." Neurologist Daniel Levitin wrote, "The emerging picture . . . is that ten thousand hours of practice is required to achieve the level of mastery associated with being a world-class expert - in anything."

Ten thousand hours is a staggering figure. But don't forget, we are talking about *mastery*. It shouldn't surprise us that a concept as powerful as mastery should come with a hefty price tag attached. Also, in most endeavors, the pursuit of mastery can produce fruit long before true mastery is accomplished. The idea is that a Rascal chases after mastery with a passion and a purpose, putting in the time and being willing to do the work towards greatness.

There should be no shame in hard work. Hard work is noble and good. For some reason, however, there is a certain trend in our society to shun hard work and glorify slothfulness. But complacency and laziness are unrewarding and unfulfilling. Rascals don't fall into this trap. They also don't allow busyness to serve as a replacement for focused, purposeful, hard work. They are not distracted by entertainments and lesser things. They work hard toward their purpose on a regular basis, developing more and more mastery continually, understanding the power of compounded incremental improvements over time.

Rascals realize that hard work is a great sorter. It sets them apart from the crowd. Most people are not willing to work hard toward mastery, and the Rascal automatically pulls away from the pack just by being willing to do the work. In time the incremental improvements from this work start to accumulate and soon one is being called "gifted" and "talented."

> **Rascals realize that hard work is a great sorter. It sets them apart from the crowd.**

Rest as Restoration

Being a 'workaholic,' a person so dedicated and driven by his work that he can think of nor do little else, however, is not the fulfillment of being a hard worker. It is the perversion of the concept. Rascals understand that when it is time to work it is time to work, and they set themselves diligently to the task. Conversely and importantly, they realize that when it is time to rest or play, it is time to do that with equal gusto.

Author Stephen Covey explained that the concept of "sharpening the saw" is a balanced approach to "self-renewal." This is important. Even machines need down-time and repair; and man is not a machine, but something infinitely more complex and valuable. It stands to reason then, that we need renewal and restoration even more so. We need constructive periods of repair and relaxation, where we are sharpened and renewed, restored and rebuilt.

However, this does not necessarily mean idleness. Laziness and unmotivated stagnation are not renewing, restoring, or rehabilitating; they are just the opposite. The reason is that they are a product of disorder, just as are overwork and busyness. In the diagram below, notice that there are two extremes of disorder. On the one side is

IDLENESS   **EFFECTIVENESS**   **BUSYNESS**

idleness and on the other is busyness. They are the symptoms of a life in chaos, where the person is not in control of his passions or calendar. Idleness is the squandering of the precious gift of time through the failure of motivation, focus, confidence, belief, or courage. Busyness is the tyranny of the urgent at the expense of the important, a condition where the passion for doing becomes an overwhelming, consuming fire, all of which we discussed earlier. The sweet spot for a Rascal is in the middle of the two extremes. It is effectiveness which leads to significance. This center location is occupied by the orderly life, with at least some modicum of balance and more than lip service paid to both goals and priorities. And it is best achieved by a driven Rascal who takes the time to sharpen his or her saw.

This is accomplished through restoration, or perhaps better seen as *rest*-oration. It is the rest in the scheduled down-times that allows the high achievements during the active times. A perfect analogy is an automobile race. It may appear momentarily that the driver who refuses a pit stop is gaining ground on the rest of the pack, but inevitably a blown tire, empty fuel tank, or other calamity will befall the driver who was too short-sighted to pull in periodically for repairs and prevention. Meanwhile, the drivers whose cars received a brief respite from the race will finish strong and ahead. So too goes life. Those who enjoy regularly scheduled down-time, who deliberately repair their frazzled nerve-endings, will finish stronger and ahead of workaholics every time.

There are many ways restoration can be accomplished. The key is that these moments are effective at restoring one to his or her fighting strength. They may be long or short, they may involve time with loved ones or in seclusion, but they should be regularly scheduled and periodic. Reading, praying, thinking, and relaxing are all suggested as effective salves. Peace and quiet also work wonders. Elton Trueblood wrote, "A public man, though he is necessarily available at many times, must learn to hide. If he is always available, he is not worth enough when he is available."

The Disposition of Attitude

It has often been said, "Attitude is everything." Author John Maxwell, however, offers a great distinction: "Attitude is not everything; rather, attitude is the difference maker."

Having a positive mental attitude could be summed up with the statement, "It's not what happens, it's how you respond." To respond is to react with maturity, with an attitude focused upon the silver lining among the storm clouds, with a belief that "this too shall pass," and an overriding optimism that says "as long as this doesn't kill me, I will be just fine!"

Filmmaker Tyler Perry is no stranger to managing his response to challenges. The son of a verbally and physically abusive father,

Perry changed his name to disassociate himself with the man who had inflicted so much pain. As a troubled kid, Tyler dropped out of school at age 16. He eventually returned and obtained his G.E.D., and then struggled to make films relevant to an audience he felt was largely missed by mainstream Hollywood: middle-class African Americans. His first movie, *Diary of a Mad Black Woman*, received harsh criticism on the Internet. The viewing public felt differently, however, and the project turned out to be a smash hit, grossing over $50 million. Perry has since written, directed, produced, and starred in many more successful films, has been featured on Oprah and 60 Minutes, and has received a smattering of other awards and recognition. Perry's attitude of overcoming was critical to his success.

Martha Washington said, "I am still determined to be cheerful and happy, in whatever situation I may be; for I have also learned from experience that the greater part of our happiness or misery depends upon our dispositions, and not upon our circumstances." Notice that Mrs. Washington used the word *determined*. She was cheerful and happy because she was *determined* to be. Having a positive attitude is a decision. The second truth embedded in her statement is that

> **Anyone can be positive when things are going well. It takes a winner to find the bright side of a dismal situation.**

circumstances should not determine attitude. Anyone can be positive when things are going well. It takes a winner to find the bright side of a dismal situation.

Having a positive attitude also comes from preparedness, hard work, and dedication. Once someone has committed fully to a project or undertaking, it is easier to have a positive attitude because of the confidence that comes from effort and preparation. In this light, a positive attitude is seen not only as a decision in spite of circumstances, but a perspective earned through the correct efforts.

Reinforcing attitude with strivings in the right direction completes a powerful circle of positive.

Having a positive, unquenchable attitude, however, is different than being a blind optimist. Ignoring the facts or sticking one's head in the sand with a cheerful heart is like smiling while going bankrupt. Nothing is accomplished by such buffoonery. Having a positive attitude doesn't preclude seeing things realistically, confronting brutal reality, or any other number of assessments required by a Rascal. It merely means that efforts won't suffer self-sabotage from an immature attitude, and mighty obstacles will be no match for a truly ambitious will.

Lou Holtz, one of the most successful college football coaches in history, said, "Ability is what you're capable of doing. Motivation determines what you do. Attitude determines how well you do it."

I Won't Until

As we discussed, long-term vision gives one a point on the horizon at which to aim. Delayed gratification is the self-denial required to get there. Success just simply cannot be had without paying the price of delayed gratification. In fact, the greater the desired reward, the greater the delay required.

> **The greater the desired reward, the greater the delay required.**

There are no free lunches. There are no shortcuts to the top, and if there ever were, it would not represent true success and certainly wouldn't last. One only has to think of "flash in the pan" geniuses or "one hit wonders" as proof.

I am reminded of the country song with the lyrics; "I made a wish upon a star, that I could drive a brand new car, I got tired of wishing, so I stole one." This is the exact opposite of delayed gratification. The burn to have something right now can lead to pragmatism, compromises, and damaging short cuts. If something is worth having it is worth *earning*. Imagine people's debt pictures if they were all taught this concept from birth!

Perhaps the best thought process for delayed gratification is, "be willing to give up what you have in the moment for what you really want in the future." What we settle for now is usually quite inferior to what we could have accomplished over the long haul.

This concept should come with a warning, however. Some people can get so carried away with living for tomorrow that they don't live in the moment. The Bible says, "sufficient for the day is the evil thereof." So, we should be careful not to violate the spirit of drinking deep from the cup of each day the Lord has given us, making each one count. Part of this, of course, is in toiling for our long term visions and over-riding dreams for the future. But part of it must involve living in the moment, being "present" with the people around us, loving our spouses and families while we are blessed to have them in our lives, serving others, giving time and attention to those in need, and, yes, we guess it's okay to smell a rose or two along the way.

Delayed gratification is not so much about *living* in the future as it is about *working toward* a brighter future, making sure the things we do with current time represent good stewardship of that time. After all, the days of our lives are a gift from God. They should not be wasted. In fact, the Bible teaches believers in Christ to lay up treasures in heaven by the things we do with our time here on earth. That is the ultimate application of long term vision and delayed gratification!

Playing Hurt

Health is a gift we often take for granted until it is compromised. When sick or ill, we hark back to the healthful days with longing; yearning to feel better again and regain our former vitality. None of us is going to be healthy forever. All will experience sickness and debilitation, to different degrees, to be sure. And to be clear, there are significant, debilitating illnesses which will quite literally take a Rascal out of his game for a period, and in extreme cases, permanently. But that doesn't mean we can't have a good attitude in the midst of the toil and realize that for a vast majority of afflictions, we will simply have to tough it out and press through it. Truth be told, many of the great achievements throughout the ages have been done by Rascals who simply had to tough it out through sickness, pain, discomfort, or whatever. When all else fails, toughness alone can be a powerful weapon to keep one in the field.

There is an interesting concept I've discovered by watching champions of all kinds: *winners learn to play hurt.* Everyone experiences sickness and pain, heartache and hurt feelings, brokenness and despair. Pestilence, hunger, disease, sickness, and injury have plagued humanity since the fall. These facts are true for rich and poor alike. The famous, lucky, beautiful and gifted all suffer as do the obscure, unlucky, ugly and average. In fact, in light of that truth, these superficial labels start to lose their power to classify people. In the end, we are all living under the same set of human conditions where pain, suffering and setbacks are just a way of life.

Rascals understand these rules of the game and learn to press on regardless. In a literal illustration, top level professional athletes learn to continue the season with wrapped injuries and pain-killers. Sitting in chill tubs or massage rooms after the games, they work through the pain to ready their bodies to perform again. Most sports are played by athletes with injuries and damaged bodies.

I will never forget a particular National Football League game in Texas years ago. The Dallas Cowboys were aiming to make it to Super Bowl XXVIII and playing a late season game at home against the New York Giants. Home field advantage for the playoffs was on the line and the Giants were giving the Cowboys a rough time of it. It looked bleak for the Cowboys when in the second quarter, star running back Emmitt Smith went down hard on the frozen surface and separated his left shoulder. The pain was evident in his face. Smith went off the field drooping his shoulder and wincing. Surprisingly, though, Smith came back into the game. He ran the ball again and got tackled hard. Slow to get up, Smith made his way back to the huddle for another play. Smith ran the ball or caught passes again, and again, and again. Each time it appeared it was all he could do just to get back up. Somehow, though, Emmitt Smith managed to carry the ball *just one more time.* Said Smith years afterward, "I'm in the huddle saying to myself, 'No pain, no pain,' I'm just talking to myself, 'no pain,' and tears are rolling out of my eyes, I'm trying to convince myself there's no pain, but I was feeling all the pain!" Teammate Michael Irving said of Smith's resilient play that day, "He stood up and played, I mean he just played and played and played. I've never seen a performance like that!" The statistics say it all. That afternoon, Emmitt Smith had the ball for 42 of the Cowboys' 70 offensive plays, with 32 runs for 170 yards and 10 catches for 62 more. The Cowboys defeated the New York Giants that day, securing home field advantage for a playoff run that would indeed see them win the Super Bowl.

The converse of this type of performance might be called "loser's limp." We've probably all seen it before: a defensive football player gets beat on a play, gives chase to the offensive player carrying the ball toward the end-zone, then upon seeing that the chase is futile, pulls up with a feigned injury as an excuse.

In life, people can choose to either *play hurt* or adopt a *loser's limp.* A loser's limp involves finding some excuse, any excuse, to explain away the lack of success. It's as if these people are searching for an explanation good enough to get them off the hook. And in fact, when it comes to choosing not to succeed, any excuse will do. It is one thing to make excuses for lack of performance to others, and that is bad enough. But the saddest excuse is the one a person sells to himself. Unfortunately, many will work very hard to convince others of the excuse they have chosen to adopt for themselves. The only problem is that any *excuse* they have for not accomplishing something has already been used by somebody else as the very *reason* for accomplishing it! The difference is whether or not someone is willing to *play hurt*!

I Will Until

If any worthwhile dream requires a long term vision and delayed gratification, it stands to reason that perseverance will be necessary, and in droves. Somehow, Rascals are able to hang on long after others are shaken off. And sometimes, after they themselves have experienced significant setbacks.

Rascals are able to hang on long after others are shaken off.

In 1835, Thomas Carlyle had finally completed his book *French Revolution*. It was to be first in a series of three volumes, a massive and ambitious work of scholarship. When tackling an immense project, as many a writer is familiar, the first part is often the most difficult. Overcoming inertia can be intimidating and exhausting. This was certainly true for Carlyle in this case. That first volume had been a struggle. For over two years Carlyle had researched, organized, collected, studied, and finally written it. He had lost sleep, his nerves were frazzled, and his finances were in dismal shape. The book had been a wrestling match, but would surely soon pay off.

Carlyle was good friends with John Stuart Mill, the famous philosopher and fellow writer. When Mill offered to read the manuscript and provide his thoughts, Carlyle consented with pleasure. One can only imagine the scene when, days later, Mill inquired as to whether Carlyle had retained a back-up copy. When Carlyle answered that he had not, Mill explained that his housekeeper had inadvertently thrown the book into the fire with some old newspapers. It was entirely destroyed. Even the research Carlyle had done was gone, as he had thrown it all away upon completion of the manuscript.

The next morning he wrote in his journal: "I will not quit the game while the faculty is given me to try playing. Oh, that I had faith! Oh, that I had! Then were there nothing too hard or heavy for me. Cry silently, to thy inmost heart to God for it. Surely He will give it thee. At all events, it is as if my invisible schoolmaster had torn my copybook when I showed it, and said, 'No, boy! Thou must write it better.' What can I, sorrowing, do but obey - obey and think it the best?"

With this determination, Carlyle sat at his desk and began to write once again. He was tired, stressed, and in financial straights, but he wrote, and wrote, and wrote. For two years he valiantly forced his way up that same old hill of inertia he had already once climbed. And there, atop that hill, Carlyle planted the flag of perseverance for all writers and strivers to see forevermore. He not only re-wrote his initial volume, but finished volumes II and III as well. And to this day, *French Revolution* is considered one of the master works on the period. Finding the strength to build something of magnificence is incredible enough the first time. But to summon the character to do it again is nearly beyond belief.

The ability to persevere through challenges and obstacles is a matter of strength, will, and focus. A Rascal keeps his or her eye upon the prize, hangs on tight, and refuses to let go. No matter what turbulence hits, Rascals are tough enough to stay the course.

One trick I have used throughout the years is to encourage myself by stating repeatedly in the face of some challenge, "Doesn't matter, doesn't matter, doesn't matter, I'm still hitting my goal!" Remember, the pain of regret is usually larger than the pain of hanging in there, so avoid regret by growing your mental toughness. Realize that no great thing was ever accomplished without overcoming struggle. In fact, every success story has the same progression: "Dream, struggle, victory." It is important to notice the order of those words. First a dream. Then a struggle. It must be a natural law that struggle always follows the advent of a real dream. This is because it is in the striving after worthwhile goals and dreams that we become better, and *who* we become is at least as important as *what* we achieve. Therefore, in the very nature of success lies a secret to greatness. But finally, notice that victory always follows struggle. Without a *test* we don't get a *testimony*. No pain, no gain. No guts, no glory. And, a popular one with Rascals everywhere: no guts, no *story*.

> **When Rascals feel as if they can't hang on any longer, they remember the reason they hung on so long in the first place!**

When Rascals feel as if they can't hang on any longer, they remember the reason they hung on so long in the first place.

With, Through, and For People

It may seem that the species of Rascal, as we've been here describing, may be inclined to be a loner, an introvert, the type to pull out of normal society and keep to seclusion. The fact is, however, that Rascals are rather the opposite. Nothing worthwhile can be done or accomplished without the cooperation of others. While individuals can achieve some things, teams can achieve nearly anything. Great accomplishments, lasting change, and maximized impact always and of a necessity involve other people. Leadership and a life well lived are nothing but contributions into the lives of others. After all, serving others is one of the primary reasons we are here.

> **Great accomplishments, lasting change, and maximized impact always and of a necessity involve other people.**

78

So, contrary to the image of the heroic loner, riding off into the sunset to the sound of breaking hearts, the real-life Rascal is more interwoven in an intentional web of relationships. Defined as *interdependence*, it is the condition of independent strengths maximized through teamwork. It is a group of independent Rascals working together, because they know that the whole is greater than the sum of the parts. It's a little like two oxen pulling a wagon. Together they can pull a much larger load than the total of their individual maximum abilities. People, unified and aligned in common purpose, see the same type of amplified results. They can accomplish much more together than apart.

Of course, there is a lot more than pragmatics to consider when discussing relationships. Fulfillment and mental health, caring, love, service, family, friendship, mentorship, parenting, spiritual development, and the entire gamut of human interaction is involved. We don't just band together to get better results in our work, we do it because it's in our very nature. We do it because it is required for warmth, security, and the deeper and most important aspects of our lives.

Understanding the power of teams over individuals, and the importance to our well-being of healthy, meaningful human interaction, Rascals are intentional about their relationships. They realize that great relationships are one of their most valuable "possessions." Because of this, Rascals are eager and willing to invest effort into initiating and fostering tight bonds with others. All relationships require effort and input over time, mixed with a healthy dose of selflessness and caring. Of course, the entire arsenal of people skills doesn't hurt either, but the most important component of building and maintaining lasting relationships is a good heart. Open and honest

> **Great relationships are like gardens, they only prosper when tended, but neglected they go to weeds.**

dealings, consistency, and depth of connection are fundamental in forging bonds that will last and serve both parties. These pieces, fused together during the passage of time, are the fibers of relationship. Rascals realize that great relationships are like gardens, they only prosper when tended, but neglected they go to weeds.

Another analogy for relationships is a fuel tank. Builders of strong relationships understand that people have 'love tanks,' like fuel tanks, that need filling. Building a friendship requires deposits into the other person's tank. Over time there will be a surplus of goodwill so that, in a time of friction or challenge, even if a withdrawal (or negative experience) happens, the other person still feels fulfilled by the relationship and the bond remains. Too many withdrawals, however, empties the tank and results in strained or broken relations. Intentional relationship builders are mindful to fill other people's tanks all the time.

Networks carefully constructed over time are powerful, and they allow for the amassment of force toward a common goal. Rascals should feel emboldened and empowered by them. They should double their efforts at building relationships that will not only be productive, but deep and meaningful, understanding that their biggest contributions in life will be with, through, and for people.

To Know and Not Do

In the movie *Scent of a Woman,* Al Pacino stars as a blind man named Mr. Slade. At the end of the movie Mr. Slade gives a compelling speech defending a young man named Charlie, played by actor Chris O'Donnell. Charlie refuses to snitch on his classmates and is in danger of being expelled from his prestigious school. The hypocrisy is too much for Slade and he stands in defiance of the hearing committee and explains, "I always knew what the right path was. *Without exception,* I *knew*. But I never took it. You know why? Because it was too [darn] hard!" His point was that young Charlie not only knew the right path to take, the one of integrity, but he also had the character to *take* it. That's the difference between a true Rascal and the rest. Confucius said, "To know what is right and not do it is the worst cowardice."

Everyone may be familiar with the basic principles discussed in this chapter, but it is a rare, exceptional person that actually *lives* them. It is an un-crowded, narrow path, populated only by Rascals.

Tank Man

The protests had gone on for seven weeks. What began as mourning for the loss of a national leader, Hu Yaobang, grew into a gigantic demonstration known to the world as the Tiananmen Square Protests of 1989. Yaobang had been a popular figure among students and intellectuals, standing for the concepts of free markets and democracy in a communist nation. At one point at the peak, the demonstrations were attended by more than one million people.

Having seen enough, the Chinese government addressed the situation by sending in the military. Throughout the course of dispelling the demonstrators, many people were killed and arrested. An unknown number of others were later rounded up and executed. In the typical fashion of tyrannical regimes, the outside world has no complete set of confirmed facts regarding the total killed, their names, or the charges against them. There is not even any information about the most famous man of the incident, the "Tank Man." All we know about him is what was shown through the camera lenses of reporters on the scene, who had to smuggle their film out of the country before what happened could be seen by the outside world.

On June 4, 1989, as a distant line of armored tanks made their way through the square, just days after other tanks had been seen driving over cars and crushing civilians, one man stood fast. He held a bag of some sort in each hand, and aligned himself with the obvious path of the oncoming tanks. As the tanks reached him they stopped. For a moment a silent stand-off ensued. Then, the man climbed up onto the tank and appeared to be attempting to talk to those inside. At one point, a man inside the tank stuck his head out of the top hatch and spoke to the protester. A moment later, as the tanks started to roll away, the man again placed himself in front of them. Another stand-off ensued. This time, men in blue uniforms emerged from a crowd of onlookers and took the protester away. There are no confirmed reports of what happened next, although rumors are rampant. The Chinese government has never been able to produce the man, and claims to be unable to state whether or not he was executed.

Although so little is known about this man, there is a lot that we *do* know. We know he was courageous. We know he believed strongly in stopping the tanks that represented a repressive government. We know he used a non-violent method to do it. And we know that his example ignited the enthusiasm of Rascals around the world for the concept of freedom from tyranny. The Tank Man, as he has been called, became an international symbol of the small standing up to the big, of the oppressed standing up to the bully, and of the defiant standing up to the enslaver. We may never know exactly what motivated him, but we can all be motivated *by* him. We may never know what happened to *him*, but we know what happened to *many around the world* as a result of his stand. Tank Man represented the flame of justice burning inside the breasts of Rascals everywhere.

CHAPTER 3

The Nemesis

The qualities we have thus far been considering are admirable and inspiring. However, life is always quick to offer its counterpoints. Rascals are violently opposed at every step. Best-selling author Steven Pressfield has formalized a name for the sum-total of all forces obstructing the high achiever: Resistance. Recently, however, I found another way to describe this opposing entity.

Introducing: Obstaclès

Obstaclès was born during a public speech I was giving in Southfield, Michigan. It was during a time when I had been reading a lot about the Persian and Peloponnesian wars, struggling, as most students likely do, with Greek pronunciations. As I wrote the word "obstacles" on the board, my Greek-saturated mind saw the word as ob-STOCK-a-leez. In an instant a star was born!

Quite simply, Obstaclès became a catchall representative of everything wimpy and unworthy inside each of us. He is powerful and relentless, low-down and shifty, a villain in the classic vein. His cartoon character persona, originally created to shine light on his craftiness, has been cleverly turned upside as he seeks to make himself seem harmless and nonsensical. It has oft been said that the greatest trick the Devil ever pulled was to convince people that he didn't exist. So don't be fooled; Obstaclès strategy is as serious as it is subtle, as effective as it is obscure.

Fear Itself

Fear heads the list of Obstaclès' deadliest and most commonly used strategies. It is his weapon of mass destruction, or rather, his weapon of *dream* destruction. This weapon is so effective it is frequently used to keep a Rascal from even beginning the journey toward success and significance. There is no way to count the number of would-be Rascals that never even started their journey because they were paralyzed by fear.

A cute acronym for fear is *false evidence appearing real.* So many times the things we fear don't come to fruition anyway, and the ones that do don't turn out to be so bad. Also, we are usually better equipped to handle them than we might have imagined. Remember that courage is not action instead of fear but in spite of fear. The best way to conquer fear is to face it.

All of this is certainly easier said than done. How many mountains haven't been climbed because of fear? How many companies were never started, books never written, movies never made, goals never accomplished, dreams never realized, fortunes never gained, relationship never initiated, all because someone gave in to fear?

There is probably not enough computing power in the world to quantify the loss fear has produced in the human experience. Obstaclès even has a special word to describe what happens when someone succumbs to fear: *wimpifying*.

Dolores Ibarruri said, "It is better to be the widow of a hero than the wife of a coward." While that is certainly extreme, it sure makes one stop and think, because whenever we give in to our fears we are playing the coward. George Bernard Shaw

> **"It is better to be the widow of a hero than the wife of a coward."**
> **- Dolores Ibarruri**

wrote, " Man gives every reason for his conduct save one, every excuse for his crimes save one, every plea for his safety save one; and that one is his cowardice."

It is at this point that it may make sense to point out that Obstaclès wears a mask. This is because he often disguises his intentions and provides just enough reason for the would-be Rascal to wimpify and justify it to himself. Most people won't admit they are giving in to their fears, instead they rationalize and justify. They not only rationalize and justify to others, but to themselves. To rationalize is to tell *rational lies*, and to justify means to whine *"just-if-I"* (as in, *just if I* had not been mistreated, etc). No matter the rationalization, justification, excuses, blame, and misdirection, cowardice is cowardice, and most people are not fooled.

It has been said that the weight of regret is tons, while the weight of courage is ounces. For those who make a habit of wimpifying when the pressure is on, of chickening out when the stakes get high, of running and hiding when times get tough, greatness will never be theirs. Instead, the pain of regret will hunt them down and haunt their dreams. Phrases like "What if?" and "If only I'd have" will run incessantly through their thoughts, and the heavy, sinking feeling of what could have been will never leave them alone. Worse, they will become known for their gutlessness. They may fool many people most of the time, but they will never fool the truly courageous. Cowards are known by those they have let down.

I know this sounds harsh. But the truth is often a bitter pill. The world has enough cowards and fakers already. These are people that look the part, say the right things, and beat their chest from safe cover, but as soon as the ammunition is real they duck and run. As Rousseau said, "The greatest braggarts are usually the biggest cowards." I would rather appear a little reckless, let people think I'm a little crazy, push the edge a little hard, and err on the side of being a Rascal than *ever* wander too close to the walk of cowards. What the world is crying out for is men and women of character and courage, who will learn to face their fears and do the right thing no matter what, who won't make excuses, blame others, or hide behind convoluted rationale.

> **What the world is crying out for is men and women of character and courage, who will learn to face their fears and do the right thing no matter what, who won't make excuses, blame others, or hide behind convoluted rationale.**

On August 14, 1961 construction of the Berlin Wall was begun. The Becker brothers of East Berlin felt an enormous fear as they watched it being constructed less than thirty yards from their home. Twice they and some of their family members began an escape attempt across the barbed wire field, and twice they were turned back by bone-shattering fear, seconds away from being captured by heavily armed Volkspolizei (People's Police). The youngest brother, Bruno, haphazardly began the process of digging a tunnel from their basement, but was stopped by the rest of the family who thought it too dangerous. After some discussion, however, the group decided that freedom *was* worth the risk, and a more elaborate plan for tunneling was decided upon. Their dream was bigger than their fear. After days and days of digging, including elaborate dirt disposal techniques, the stringing of lights, watching for guards, deflecting inquiries of neighbors, and a few cave-ins, the far edge of the tunnel was finally beyond the furthest fence. Crawling just three feet below the feet of patrolling police, twenty-eight men, women, and children overcame their fears of darkness, confined spaces, cave-ins, and capture, and crawled from tyranny to freedom. Most of us will never find it necessary to tunnel to freedom from Communist oppression, but we will have fears that will just as effectively discourage our freedoms and greatest aspirations. If the Becker family could face their fears, we can face ours.

The best way to overcome fears is to take action. Set short term goals that put pressure on achievement in the here and now. Get in touch with your motivations and stoke the flames of your own hunger. Re-

> **The best way to overcome fears is to take action.**

member, hunger for success is a discipline that must be exercised like a muscle to get stronger, and the stronger that muscle, the easier fears are to overcome. Also, pushing through one's comfort zone builds a kind of momentum. The more one does it the easier it becomes. Confidence builds and memory of victory emboldens and enables further attempts. Gradually, the outer boundaries of the comfort zone are pushed further away and what was uncomfortable yesterday becomes normal today. It is in this way that most great achievements were accomplished. They weren't made by a moon-shot or a big lucky break; more likely and more often they were the product of a multitude of incremental steps of courage over time.

The ancient Latin proverb says, *fortes fortuna adiuvat*, which loosely translated is, "fortune favors the bold." Rascals are bold. They face their fears and don't fall for the subterfuges of Obstaclès. Rascals know that there will always be a thousand reasons why they can't do something, but all they need to find is *one* reason why they *can*.

I Doubt It

Another potent weapon in Obstaclès' arsenal is doubt. Even though a person may be plenty courageous, he or she may still harbor doubt. There are many kinds of doubt; doubt about one's goals, doubt about one's beliefs, doubt about one's abilities, doubt about one's judgment, etc. Some forms of doubt, in fact, are healthy. Doubt can be a safeguard on our behavior, effectively asking us before undertaking some endeavor, "Are you sure?"

The doubt wielded by Obstaclès, however, is not the healthy kind. It is, rather, the kind that destroys the foundations of greatness. This kind of doubt aims at the heart, motive, and very spirit of the Rascal. It decimates a Rascal's convictions. It seeks to knock him or her off the confident path of achievement and into the bushes of analysis and reconsideration. Again, these can be somewhat healthy in limited dosages, but Obstaclès is the master of the overdose. He deals in extremes. He knows that if he can knock a Rascal off the path once with doubt, he can likely do it again with even more doubts. He tries many flavors of doubt until he finds which mixture works best, then intensifies the potion with the intent of keeping the Rascal sidelined as much as possible. Time wasted analyzing and reconsidering is time lost from moving toward life goals and callings. And once the time is gone it's gone forever.

> **Time wasted analyzing and reconsidering is time lost from moving toward life goals and callings.**

Michelangelo, perhaps the world's greatest artist, will not be remembered for his martial abilities. His home city of Florence was a nation-state in its own right, and, for that matter, one which had incurred the wrath of an alliance between the Pope and Holy Roman Emperor Charles V. It was feared the city would be attacked, and the young war hawks of the town had succeeding in whipping up enthusiasm for armed resistance. A militia was formed and money was appropriated for mercenaries. As was often the case, artists were considered craftsmen, and assumed to be capable of a broad range of vocations. In that spirit, Michelangelo was assigned oversight for the construction of the city's defenses. Christopher Hibbert wrote, "Michelangelo waited to see the works almost completed, then lost his nerve and fled from the city. A few days later he returned, and though not reinstated in his former responsible position, his behavior was attributed to his artistic temperament and he was forgiven." Michelangelo had given in to self-doubt about the ability of his defenses to do their job, was afraid of being blamed for their failure, and perhaps experienced a lapse in courage, as well.

Doubt is an extremely toxic poison because it infects convictions, the very source of a Rascal's success. As we've already discussed, a Rascal's convictions are crucial. Doubt weakens a Rascal's resolve by chipping away at his or her foundational beliefs.

> **Doubt is an extremely toxic poison because it infects convictions, the very source of a Rascal's success.**

One of the most damaging areas of doubt is self-doubt. This is the condition where the Rascal loses confidence in him or her self. This is a very dangerous malady and a tough situation to fix. Once someone loses belief in his ability to achieve something, he loses the drive to attempt it. Obstaclès knows that people will only do what they believe they *can* do.

Another dangerous form of doubt is doubt in one's dreams and goals, as in, "Are these really worth achieving?" or "Are these even possible for me to attain?" This can happen through any number of channels, including (again) self-doubt, or a lack of focus on the foundational principles and beliefs that produced the Rascal's inspiration in the first place. Therefore, one of the strongest defenses a Rascal has against Obstacle's weapon of doubt is to become a self-directed learner, always growing in character, belief, and conviction in those beliefs.

Doubt in others is also deadly. Obstaclès loves to do nothing better than break up a team, relationship, or marriage by sowing seeds of doubt in one person about another. Cowards, like birds who spread seeds through their excrement, play a big part in this game. They gossip and whisper and exhibit passive-aggressive behavior, talking behind people's backs and wedging doubt into the bonds of trust, shoots from their sowing sprouting up everywhere. The Bible calls it, "Sowing seeds of discord among the brethren (Proverbs 6:19)," and says that it is one of the six things the Lord hates, one of the seven that are an abomination to Him. Obstaclès knows that almost nothing is as damaging to a team as doubt about the leadership.

Finally, doubt in the results of one's efforts is also debilitating. When we come to a point where we think what we do doesn't matter, or doubt that it is worth our time, we immediately slow down in our efforts and maybe stop altogether. Obstaclès loves this one, because this leads directly into frustration and discouragement. Obstaclès encourages his victims to doubt the very path they've chosen, giving them rearward glances at their past life and enticing them back into the lure of mediocrity. "It wasn't so bad back where you used to be," he whispers, "You're not really the type to be chasing so hard after goals and dreams," or "Being a couch potato was actually fun, don't you remember?" These and myriad other doubt-starters just like them will be hurled at the Rascal on his journey. Others take the angle of: "Are you sure what you're doing is going to pay off?" or "Are you sure this is the right thing to be doing with your time?" or even doubt that appeals to one's ego such as, "Are you sure you want to waste your time doing this? Aren't you too good for this endeavor?" Like a chess master, Obstaclès has many moves and compound maneuvers at his disposal to confound the would-be Rascal with doubt.

Winners make decisions *to do* something quickly, *to quit* something slowly. Rascals realize that they may have doubts along their path to success, but they are slow to *un-decide*, knowing that success is usually a result of simply hanging

> **Winners make decisions *to do* something quickly, *to quit* something slowly.**

on for the long haul and having the character to persevere through moments of doubt. As with most of these weapons wielded by Obstaclès, doubt is most effectively repulsed by the *character* of the Rascal.

Confidentially Unconfident

The self-doubt discussed above plays directly upon what all of us feel to some extent or from time to time, and that is a lack of confidence and drooping self-image. Obstaclès is a master, of course, at exploiting this one.

For some reason, many people feel a niggling sense of unworthiness deep down inside. This leads to the lack of effort and "settle for" lifestyle that appears so pervasive in our society. We don't feel worthy so we don't try. We compare ourselves to others and think they are either more gifted, better positioned, more deserving, or simply luckier. We convince ourselves that to try would be futile because we aren't as good as those who are succeeding.

If comparison to others isn't deadly enough, Obstaclès is quick to remind us of our own past. "Remember that time you were made to look like a fool in front of the whole class?" "Don't forget that time she broke up with you!" "You blew the last inning in the little league championship game!" It seems Obstaclès has instant recall of our past lineage of failures and produces them just at the right time. In the face of such mounting evidence it takes a real Rascal to push forward anyway, daring to believe that if someone else made it, *anyone* can!

There are many things a Rascal can do to defeat Obstaclès' weapon of low confidence. The first is to do what we discussed earlier: visualize success regularly and clearly. Remember, the more you picture something the more likely it is to come true. Next is the action habit. The more our actions are in line with the highest picture we have of our self, the more we reinforce the belief that we *can* actually succeed. It's as if we convince our subconscious mind that we are serious and are actually going to make it this time. One of the keys to growing in confidence is to work hard enough that you *know* beyond a shadow of a doubt that you *deserve* success. Effort toward a goal has a lot to do with feeling like we deserve the goal. Realizing that we deserve it has a lot to do with our ability to finish strong.

In many ways we are who we think we are. If we put a small value on ourselves, rest assured the world will not raise our price. We must raise our own value by controlling the power of our thoughts to reinforce the positive aspects of our

> **In many ways we are who we think we are.**

self-concept. Coming to grips with the spiritual truths about who we are, why we were created, and who we can be through God's grace - gives us a confidence that is real.

One of the best calibrators of self-image I have ever encountered comes from Og Mandino's book *The Greatest Miracle in the World*. In it Mandino writes, "We are unhappy because we no longer have our self-esteem. We are unhappy because we no longer believe we are a special miracle, a special creation of God." Mandino ends his classic book with something he calls *The God Memorandum*. It is a fictitious imagining of God giving a pep-talk to human beings who have forgotten Him and how special He created each person. Following is a small portion:

"Never, in all the seventy billion humans who have walked this planet since the beginning of time has there been anyone exactly like you. Never, until the end of time, will there be another such as you. You have shown no knowledge or appreciation of your uniqueness. Yet, you are the rarest thing in the world. From your father . . . flowed countless seeds . . . more than four hundred million in number. All of them, as they swam . . . gave up the ghost and died. All except one! You. You alone persevered within the loving warmth of your mother's body, searching for your other half, a single cell from your mother so small that more than two million would be necessary to fill an acorn shell. Yet, despite impossible odds, in that vast ocean of darkness and disaster, you persevered, found that infinitesimal cell, joined with it, and began a new life. Your life . . . Two cells now united in a miracle. Two cells, each containing twenty-three chromosomes and within each chromosome hundreds of genes, which would govern every characteristic about you, from the color of your eyes to the charm of your manner, to the size of your brain. With all the combinations at my command . . . I could have created three hundred thousand billion humans, each different from the other. But who did I bring forth? You! One of a kind. Rarest of the rare. A priceless treasure, possessed of qualities in mind and speech and movement and appearance and actions as no other who has ever lived, lives, or shall live. Why have you valued yourself in pennies when you are worth a king's ransom? Why did you listen to those who demeaned you . . . and far worse, why did you believe them?"

Pride Before the Fall

Closely related to a lack of confidence in the arsenal of Obstaclès is the case of an overblown ego. It is a battering ram used in frontal assault on the progress of a Rascal. Failures of pride and/or ego occur when one asserts his or her own self-worth to the detriment of others. Obstaclès can use the failure of pride to derail even the most worthy achiever. As the Bible states, "Pride cometh before the fall."

Many in England thought the scuffle with their North American colonies should have been concluded already. A new attack, planned for the 1777 season, a major portion of which was to be led by flamboyant General "Gentleman Johnny" Burgoyne, was launched. Burgoyne's part of the overall plan was to strike down through Canada with a large force of arms and men, meeting up with other British armies making their way in from the south. The result would be a great pincer movement that would split the colonies in two and disable their united resistance.

Although Burgoyne is generally acclaimed as a decent soldier, historians are largely in agreement that he was not a good leader. His self-assurance, on topics for which he was not an expert, was the seed of his undoing. Burgoyne underestimated the time and effort required to march a large army through the wilderness, and he missed entirely the strategies of battles in woods and hills. He also failed to properly grasp the complexities of dealing with his Native American allies, which resulted in their desertion of him at a key moment. Burgoyne, instead of learning all he could about the treacherous terrain and fragile alliances of the area, assumed he knew all he needed to know. In addition, he actually published bombastic proclamations in the newspapers, promising to "execute the Vengeance of the State against the willful Outcast."

Burgoyne was badly defeated at the Battle of Saratoga, surrendering his entire army of 6,000 men. Though some of the blame must fall to his fellow commanders for failing to execute their part of the coordinated movement, much of it rests squarely on his own shoulders. He had assumed too much, believed in his own prescience too much, and had marched a glorious and well-trained army into total defeat. The ramifications of Burgoyne's loss was staggering. It gave the colonial ambassadors in France the victory they needed to convince France to enter the war on the colonial side. This ultimately turned the tide of the war.

Failures of pride sneak up on us suddenly. At first we don't take much notice of the recognition others receive, or of slights and injustices that come our way. But all of us, at some level, become susceptible to tinges of pride, hurt feelings, and the desire for prominence. This happens when we take our eyes off the larger picture of living a life of purpose, of serving others, and of sacrificing our own selfish concerns for the sake of something greater.

> **All of us, at some level, become susceptible to tinges of pride, hurt feelings, and the desire for prominence.**

Obstaclès will attack by getting the Rascal to focus on something other than his goal. "Take a look at the what that other person is accomplishing," he will jibe. "Look at the rewards *they* are receiving that *you* deserve instead. You deserve it more. You aren't being treated fairly," and on and on he goes. Seeds of such damaging thoughts are planted in our minds. If we water them with any acknowledgement whatsoever, they will sprout and begin to grow. If we ever, for even a moment, allow ourselves to become concerned about what *we* deserve, how *we* should be treated, how *our* reputation must be protected, how *we* should not be slighted, how *we* are to be respected, and the honors to which *we* think we are obligated, we have sown the seeds of our own destruction. All of this stems from an overblown concept of who we are and what we deserve, and from focusing upon ourselves.

Again, understanding the correct picture of who we are in relation to a Creator is the starting point of the defense against failures of pride. Any time we try to put ourselves on little thrones of our own, Obstaclès will easily step in and unseat us. True leaders, true achievers, true Rascals, are here to serve others, and to serve a purpose larger than themselves. The more we realize that, the more likely we are to remain grounded and humble. It is not that Rascals aren't confident, it's just that they rely on the adherence to their callings and purpose for this confidence and not upon their own exalted selves.

> **Understanding the correct picture of who we are in relation to a Creator is the starting point of the defense against failures of pride.**

A Shiny Object on the Side of the Road

Not all of Obstaclès' attacks are frontal. One of his most subtle weapons involves the diversionary tactic of distraction. Obstaclès knows this is a complex world in which we live. There are so many things to capture our attention and affection we are in constant danger of becoming sidetracked. Many a good intention has ended in obscurity, many a great leader has fallen to distraction, many a great book remains partially-written, many a musical composition is still unfinished, and many a goal has gone unachieved. These are the casualties of distraction, and their tally would fill all the ledger books in the world.

Falling victim to distraction has happened to all of us at one time or another. Take cleaning the garage as an example. We block out a few hours on a Saturday morning, put on work clothes, and head into the danger zone, ready to make a difference. At first we straighten a few things. But as we do we notice a broken wheel on a bicycle and stop to fix that. To fix the bicycle, however, we need a box-end wrench, and when we look through our tool box we realize it's a mess and immediately set about organizing it. In it we find a long-lost flashlight and attempt to turn it on, only to find the batteries dead. Obviously this needs to be fixed, and there is no time like the present. So it's back inside the house to the closet for new batteries, only to find they've all been used. At this point we make our way to the kitchen to add batteries to the shopping list, at which point we realize we are hungry, which has us rummaging around in the refrigerator. Unfailingly, at this moment our spouse walks in and says something along the lines of, "Hey, I thought you were going to clean the garage today?" This is a picture of the power of distraction to derail the accomplishment of anything, even something as simple as cleaning a garage!

The Federal Aviation Administration compiles crash statistics and analyses for pilots everywhere to study for the purpose of increasing their own safety while aloft. One condition found in many of these analyses is pilot distraction. At certain points in the flight, particularly during take-off and approach to landing, flying is a busy job. Pilots are aviating (physically controlling the plane), navigating (controlling the direction of the plane), and communicating (talking to Air Traffic Control, Flight Watch Services, and possibly other pilots). They also must deal with passengers, their own physical needs (many is the landing with a full bladder), and co-pilots. There are also weather conditions, fuel levels, airplane performance, and gauges and electronics to monitor. With all this going on, it is easy to understand how pilots could become distracted. As a result, there have been flights which missed or overshot runways, departed on the wrong runway, and even landed at the wrong airport! Distraction can be deadly to an aviator, and should illustrate the power of Obstaclès to throw an otherwise capable and highly-trained individual off track.

Distraction to an adult with a goal is a lot like a shiny object on the side of the path to a toddler. It doesn't matter what the distraction *is*, it only matters that it *glitters*. It only needs to capture the attention for an instant. That's all it takes to break focus, and broken focus leads to broken dreams.

> **Broken focus leads to broken dreams.**

There is another form of distraction involving things not fundamental to our calling. This relates to what we covered before: there are many, many *good* things we can do, but usually only one or two *great* things. Seth Godin wrote, "We fail when we get distracted by tasks we don't have the guts to quit."

Rascals fight back against Obstaclès by focusing on the great and disregarding the good. Some call this learning to *major on majors*. As legendary basketball coach Pat Riley said, "The main thing is to keep the main thing the main thing."

Doing Pretty Good

There is a disease of mediocrity in our lands these days and I think much of it springs from the soil of complacency. Obstaclès uses our very blessings against us, allowing our comforts to soften us, deaden our hunger for excellence, and stifle our ambitions. Complacency can set in at any level, resulting in the oft-heard phrase, "I'm doing pretty good." This mind-set is a time bomb, a weapon of Obstaclès set for our future destruction. It does no damage in the short term, but the weapon of complacency silently and persistently ticks down the seconds until our eventual destruction.

Understand: Rascals don't settle for 'pretty good.' Good is never good enough if better is available. Rascals are in hot pursuit of excellence and significance, not peace and affluence. Rascals don't rust out; they skid ten feet at the end!

Sometimes it is more important to be reminded than instructed. Many of the most important things we learn are things we *re-learn*! Often, battling complacency works just this way. We understand basic truths about hunger and success and significance and the pursuit of excellence, but we fall prey to our comforts and back off the throttle a bit, losing our 'edge' and slipping out of 'the zone.' We need something to jolt us out of our false-comfort and reawaken us to our calling.

Erik Weihenmayer is the blind mountain climber who has not only climbed Mt. Everest, but all seven of the world's highest peaks. Weihenmayer and his climbing team set a new world record by summiting with nineteen out of their group of twenty. Weihenmayer is an extremely humble and classy guy. He readily gives away credit to his teammates and climbing mentors. One thing above all, however, is most striking about Weihenmayer: his determination to fulfill his calling. In a world where the smallest barrier stops people from accomplishing even small things, Weihenmayer accomplishes things without sight that most people with 20-20 vision won't even attempt! Weihenmayer is forced to do these things with every bit of his ability, in spite of his disability.

The questions beg to be asked: Why do so many people, given perhaps more physical blessings than someone like Weihenmayer, do so much less with their lives? Why do most people waste their days without ever seeking that purpose for which they were built? Why don't people take more risks to pursue the ends to which their God-given talents and passions point them? Perhaps the biggest question is: "If we had been blessed with less, would we be accomplishing more?" Sure, Erik Weihenmayer has an obvious physical disability. But everyone, including Weihenmayer, has *mental* disabilities. We are all limited by pride, ego, fear, lack of confidence, laziness, passivity, indifference, and the desire for comfort. Perhaps Weihenmayer became good at overcoming his limitations because he was forced to do so in the case of his lost eyesight. The same mental toughness he developed to overcome his physical disability may have become supremely instructive in how to overcome his mental disabilities. We all need inspirational examples like Erik Weihenmayer to get us thinking, to awaken our minds to the potential that lies inside us, and to enable us to see our complacency from a proper perspective.

Obstacles can cause complacency to set in on any performer when things are going well. At such a time it is helpful to find a defeat in every victory. No matter how well things are going, nor how high the achievements, something can always be found upon which to improve. There is always a better personal best, a more excellent success to be attained. This ensures that cockiness and laziness don't set in. Of course, if things are going badly, Orrin Woodward recommends turning the saying around to: "Find a victory in every defeat." There is always hope, always a silver lining, always another chance. Look for the shards of goodness in a broken pile of scraps and hang on to that one good thing.

> **No matter how well things are going, nor how high the achievements, something can always be found upon which to improve.**

Comfort is a trap. Complacency is a disease that robs us of our best efforts. Rascals never succumb to the lures of ease, and they never give in to the temptation to think they have arrived. They force themselves to stay hungry, set higher goals, and move ahead even further, all the while taking stock of great examples of overcoming like Erik Weihenmayer. Rascals count their blessings and march those blessings into battle for a higher purpose instead of sitting on them and hording them away, understanding that their privileges are not for their pleasure, but for their purpose. As the Bible says, "To whom much is given, much is required."

Out of Character

King David of ancient Israel was monarch of one of the great kingdoms of the world. As a boy he had killed wild animals, felled the giant Goliath whom professional soldiers were scared to face, evaded state persecution by King Saul, survived by hiding out in caves and the wilderness, and was hand-selected by the profit Samuel to be the future king. As ruler he was benevolent and effective, ushering in one of the greatest and most glorious periods in Israel's history. The Bible even refers to him as a man after God's own heart. But we also learn that "in the spring when kings go to war" David was instead home napping. Awaking from that nap, defenses down, he allowed himself to be tempted by the sight of a beautiful woman on an adjacent rooftop. This led to a calamity of sins and marked the decline of his reign. Obstaclès had struck with his most deadly weapon; character failure. The use of this nuclear warhead is always devastating, and involves collateral damage in the lives of other people. With weapons of this magnitude, there is always fallout.

Character failures are real. The story of mighty king David should serve as adequate warning to all: even the best of men can fall at any time. It takes merely seconds to destroy the character years were required to build. Obstaclès understands how susceptible the human spirit is to failure, knowing also that the higher the person the mightier the fall. Therefore Rascals everywhere should be on guard, realizing that in terms of character, one never arrives. Character is a precious quantity we should continuously work to strengthen and fight to protect. Abraham Lincoln stated, "Character is like a tree and reputation like its shadow. The shadow

> The story of mighty king David should serve as adequate warning to all: even the best of men can fall at any time.

is what we think of it; the tree is the real thing." We may not be able to control our reputations, but we are entirely in charge of our character.

There are many character failures into which Obstaclès can attempt to lure the unsuspecting Rascal. Among these are ego, jealousy, pride, arrogance, selfishness, lying, adultery, stealing, lust, covetousness, gossip, envy, hatred, harboring grudges, an unforgiving spirit, addictions, cheating, win-lose maneuvers, secret lies, malicious thoughts, and many other sorts of evil. Each Rascal has his own particular weaknesses and cracks in his armor, and it doesn't take long for Obstaclès to identify them and start pecking away in the correct areas.

One way to guard against failures of character is to pretend all your actions are written in the sky. Ask yourself if what you did in the dark were known in the light, would you behave differently? Also, building a strong spiritual foundation is key. As Dwight Moody said, "The Bible will keep you from sin, or else sin will keep you from the Bible." Our character, then, is not something we are endowed with at birth. We must work hard at it. It comes from discipline. It's intentional. It is an edifice we construct, over time, with the actions and behaviors of our life. We are responsible for how sturdy that edifice becomes, and how long it stands strong.

Failures of character are extremely hard to overcome, and many such failures have knocked achievers off the path of success forever. This is because a lack of character shatters trust, and once lost, trust is one of the hardest things to regain. As the saying goes, people are "once bitten, twice shy." That doesn't necessarily mean that the situation is hopeless, but there should be no delusions that it will be easy. Trust is earned, and once spent, is bought back only at a dear price.

> **Trust is earned, and once spent, is bought back only at a dear price.**

104

In contrast, people of character are a joy to be around. They are trustworthy and refreshing. Since they are so rare they are often surrounded by friends and admirers, respected by colleagues and critics alike. This is the description of a true Rascal.

Author and political expert Peggy Noonan wrote, "In a president, character is everything. A president doesn't have to be brilliant. . . He doesn't have to be clever; you can hire clever. . . You can hire pragmatic, and you can buy and bring in policy wonks. But you can't buy courage and decency, you can't rent a strong moral sense. A president must bring those things with him. . . He needs to have, in that much maligned word, but a good one nonetheless, a 'vision' of the future he wishes to create. . . But a vision is worth little if a president doesn't have the character-- the courage and heart-- to see it through." This is not only true of a President of the United States, but for any Rascal. Character predominates all other talents and skills. Without it nothing of significance will sustain; with it almost everything else can be added unto it.

On a lighter note, perhaps the best insight on character ever given is from Ronald Reagan, who could say things as only a Rascal would: "You can tell a lot about a fellow's character by his way of eating jelly beans."

Extraordinary Popular Delusions and the Madness of Crowds

The subheading for this section, believe it or not, is a shortened version of the title of a best-selling book written a century and a half ago. The power of crowds over individual behavior is a highly documented and long studied phenomenon. Interesting dynamics emerge from such studies; like the fact that a mugging victim is more likely to be saved by a lone observer than if the crime were witnessed by a crowd. The crowd dynamics that take over apparently cause everyone to assume that "someone else" will handle the situation. When facing such dilemmas alone, however, a person is more likely to play the hero.

This kind of crowd power manifests itself in many ways, large and small. It leads to fashion, political correctness, language vernaculars and colloquialisms, trends, buying patterns, and even educational and career choices. In short, people are influenced by other people. For leaders such as Rascals, this is good news. But it also carries an underside. It also means that people are susceptible to people-pleasing, even sometimes when it might not be healthy.

Pontius Pilate was Prefect of the Roman province of Judea during the time of Jesus. When the religious leaders demanded Jesus' crucifixion for supposedly blaspheming the name of God, Pilate was hesitant, seeing no evidence himself justifying capital punishment. From his perspective, there was nothing under Roman law concerning minor disputes within the Jewish religion. The Sanhedrin, the upper echelon of the Jewish religious power structure, demanded satisfaction. Pilate, therefore, looked for justification that might be used under Roman law. He inquired as to whether Jesus claimed to be the "King of the Jews," as the Sanhedrin had charged, and therefore a political threat to Roman authority. Even on that point, after a brief interrogation, Pilate declared, "I find no fault in him." The Sanhedrin were adamant, however, countering with a veiled threat, saying, "If thou let this man go, thou art not Caesar's friend: whosoever maketh himself a king speaketh against Caesar." Pilate then reached for the Passover tradition of releasing a prisoner of the people's choice as his way out of responsibility. He offered to release either a prisoner named Barabbas, or Jesus. The small crowd there assembled had been coached by the Sanhedrin to shout for Jesus' crucifixion. Perplexed, Pilate released Barabbas and set in motion the crucifixion of Jesus, symbolically washing his hands in water and saying, "I am innocent of the blood of this just person: see ye to it."

Many scholars have analyzed this most important passage in history, attempting to discern the motivation behind Pilate's decision.

Did he give in to the pressure of the crowd? Or was he primarily interested in making sure good reports about his rule over the Jews made it back to Rome? Both explanations may contain some merit, but the overall impression of Pilot caving in to the pressure of the religious elite and the chanting crowd has remained for two millennia.

It is a fact that people are swayed and persuaded by the pressure of approval and acceptance of other people. By now it is probably no surprise to learn that Obstaclès also uses this little truth of human nature against Rascals. As if thrown from a catapult, it is hurled over the walls of a Rascal's defense. Understanding that even Rascals have a deep desire to be loved and appreciated, Obstaclès will tempt them into Behavior Unbecoming of a Rascal (B.U.R.). By very definition, a Rascal is someone who goes the opposite way of the crowd, standing boldly defiant against the power of *they*, plowing his own path and following his own calling. This doesn't mean, however, that even a Rascal isn't tempted to run along side the sheep from time to time.

> **It is a fact that people are swayed and persuaded by the pressure of approval and acceptance of other people.**

"Aw, come on!" *they* will say. "Everybody is doing it," or, "You work too hard, don't you want to have some fun like the rest of us?" or "You've been working so long and hard and haven't made it yet; you need a break," or "You think you can accomplish *that*?" "Where do you think you're going?" or "Do you think you're better than the rest of us?" or "Who do you think you are dreaming big dreams?" The details don't matter. Whatever Obstaclès can use to throw a Rascal off his game will definitely be attempted. The weapon is always deployed along the same line: the desire to please the crowd, to fit in, to be somebody (as if the blessing of the crowd had anything to do with bestowing credibility). Rascals, however, are not fooled. They know the reasons they do what they do, and they run their race whether there are crowds cheering or not. They also understand that to have different results in life they need to think and act differently. Rascals listen to the people who have the results they want in life, not the masses who are content accomplishing nothing of significance. As Bill Cosby said, "I don't know the key to success, but the key to failure is trying to please everybody."

> "I don't know the key to success, but the key to failure is trying to please everybody."
> - Bill Cosby

Show Me the Money

Obstaclès knows there is nothing like the stress brought on by financial troubles, and he wields this fact like a subversive weapon. It erodes the underpinnings of strength and eliminates the resources a Rascal often needs to perform. For some reason, money problems have the ability to pervade even the toughest resolves, reducing giants to worrying wimps. Obstaclès has used the power of financial pain to throw many a would-be Rascal off the path of success, destroy otherwise strong marriages, and split apart friendships and partnerships. The more focused a person is on his own material well-being, the more susceptible he is to the attack of financial worry. We can learn a lot about our true priorities by the way we respond to a lack of money.

> We can learn a lot about our true priorities by the way we respond to a lack of money.

An anonymous quote states, "The real measure of your wealth is how much you'd be worth if you lost all your money."

The collapse of the sub-prime mortgage market in late 2008 was the culmination of greed, ignorance, and financial irresponsibility all tied into one. Mortgages written to people who couldn't qualify were bundled and sold on the open market. This worked because they were ostensibly backed by the strength and power of the United States government, and were therefore assumed to be a safe investment. This "derivative market" was a fun game while the cards stayed in place. But when the economy slowed and marginal homeowners started defaulting on their loans, the house of cards collapsed.

What happened? A thorough explanation would take a book of its own. One aspect of the crisis, however, fed upon people's desire to live above their means. People without the financial wherewithal were granted loans that were too big in comparison to their ability to pay them back. The temptation to buy that beautiful new home was just too much for some to resist. Thousands of people over-reached because their bankers told them they could. Besides, people had largely been misled into believing their homes were an asset and that property "goes up in value over time." As soon as housing appreciation turned and went backward into depreciation, and at the same time people began losing jobs and the ability to make their payments, an avalanche of foreclosures hit the market. Billions in investment money was lost, but perhaps more painfully, thousands of homeowners were bankrupted. For anyone who has ever been "upside down" in their home (owing more money on it than it is worth for sale on the open market), there is a special sense of exasperation. The type of personal financial catastrophe we saw in the housing-bubble pop, repeated in thousands of cases across the country, had an obvious negative effect on the economy. The mess is still being mopped up, and people all over are still struggling to emerge from the fog of financial failure. It would be impossible to account for the lost health, stress, worry, and opportunity cost of things not accomplished because of this financial hurricane in the lives of so many.

Financial pressure affects people differently. Some get paralyzed by it; unable to take action to rectify their problems, because they spend so much time simply considering their mess. Others over-react in near panic, sacrificing their dreams and long-term aspirations on the altar of expedience and immediate pain-relief. People lose sleep, get in bad moods, disregard their families, stop volunteering in the community, and basically get off track in their lives, all because of money. We can likely all point to someone who has experienced breakdowns mentally, in their health, and in their relationships because of financial trauma. Obstaclès relishes all of these side effects of money pain, and does his best to fan their flames. It is subversive weaponry at its worst!

Losing Heart

Obstaclès is fond of sustained attacks of frustration, which ultimately lead to discouragement. Like victims of a relentless air attack, Rascals are sent scurrying for cover amid the wail of sirens. Discouragement is what happens when a Rascal loses belief. This occurs when a Rascal grows weary in well doing, misses goals, loses momentum, and sustains set-back after set-back to the point of exasperation. The sustained assault of difficulty finally takes its damaging toll.

Long before the U.S. military officially showed up in Viet Nam, "advisors" were on the ground and involved in joint operations with the South Vietnamese. In 1963 one of these men, James N. Rowe, was a special forces officer who was captured and imprisoned in horrible conditions for five years. Malnourished, sick with dysentery, afflicted by a skin fungus, and held in constant confinement, Rowe describes that these only comprised part of his tortuous captivity. One of the most grueling aspects was the forced "educational" sessions he had to endure. After years of relentless communist and socialist indoctrination, Rowe was still defiant. He later wrote:

"Political indoctrination during 1966 and 1967 continued as before. . . For the first time we learned of the antiwar movement in the United States. . . [the North Vietnamese enemy] reported protests on campuses across the [U.S.], which we took as normal exaggeration, but it stayed with us . . . [The enemy] conducted several classes [for us] on 'the just cause of the revolution and the injustice of the U.S. dirty war of aggression.' [They] always claimed that [none of their] troops were present in South Vietnam, and there were specific instructions to the [prison guards and indoctrination teachers] to deny any link with the Communist Party of Vietnam, headed by Ho Chi Minh. This link was the first thing an American prisoner looked for to justify his own beliefs. If the [enemy] could convince him that a Communist-inspired insurgency didn't exist, the rest of the [prisoner of war's] beliefs could be attacked. Had I not understood some Vietnamese, I might have missed hearing the daily political classes attended by the guards in which the doctrine *Marx-it*, *Le-nin-it*, was taught to even the youngest. It was incongruous to hear the cadre teaching Marxist philosophy to the guards, yet denying any connection with communism when talking with Americans. The fact that the cadre felt the need to lie strengthened my conviction that I was right in my beliefs."

Thankfully Rowe was able to make a remarkable escape, saved in a nick of time by American helicopters. His words are very illustrative of how a person becomes discouraged, a fact understood by the North Vietnamese as the basis for their propaganda campaign. Their goal was to align themselves with the peace movement in the United States and show the world that the U.S. didn't belong in the war. If they could "turn" a few American military prisoners and get them to "confess" their "capitalist-imperialist crimes," it would feed the flames of the resistance movement back in the U.S.. Their strategy didn't work with Major Rowe. Even though, after draining Rowe's physical reserves down to the breaking point, the North Vietnamese systematically attacked the props of Rowe's belief system, he understood just enough Vietnamese to find small evidence of their lies and to confirm his own beliefs. These beliefs kept him from cracking long after others had given in to total discouragement and despair.

Obstaclès knows that discouragement is very dangerous to success because it tempts the Rascal to consider quitting, thinking there is little hope and concluding that all efforts are fruitless. Just as with Major Rowe, discouragement is often a lie. Things are rarely as bad as they seem, and usually a little better perspective or small piece of new evidence is all that's needed to restore faith. It comes down to a Rascal's belief and the reasons that support that belief.

Mother Teresa

Born in 1910 Agnese Gonxhe Bojaxhiu in Uskub, Ottoman Empire, she was the youngest child in a family from Albania. At age eight, when her father died, she began attending a Roman Catholic church. By age twelve she was convinced her life would be a religious one, and she became fascinated by stories of missionaries. In 1931 she took her first religious vows and chose the name Teresa for herself after the patron saint of missionaries, Therese de Lisieux. In 1946 she received what she called her "call within the call" to leave the convent and serve the poor.

It was a courageous and wild decision, one that would throw her into hunger and doubt. She had absolutely no income and had to resort to begging for supplies and food. In the early days she was constantly tempted to return to the relative comfort of the convent, but she allowed her compassion for the poor to drive her onward.

In 1950 she founded the Missionaries of Charity with the purpose of caring for "the hungry, the naked, the homeless, the crippled, the blind, the lepers, all those people who feel unwanted, unloved, uncared for throughout society, people that have become a burden to the society and are shunned by everyone." Her charity grew from a tiny concern in a Calcutta, India, into an enormous, world-wide organization.

In 1952 she opened her first Home for the Dying. Next she opened a home for those suffering from leprosy, as well as several leprosy clinics throughout Calcutta. In 1955, her Missionaries of Charity opened the Children's home of the Immaculate Heart as a home for orphans. By the 1960s the Missionaries of Charity were running hospices, leper homes, and orphanages across India, and soon thereafter began expanding similar operations around the globe.

All of this was wonderful in a way. With such a growing organization focused upon the lowest strata of existence, Mother Teresa and her Missionaries of Charity garnered international fame. She was featured in books and a documentary. She began receiving honors from around the world. She also received some scathing criticism that would follow her consistently throughout the rest of her life.

Caring for the poor was fine, according to her critics, but they had problems with her methods. Some attacked the conditions in her hospices, others attacked her treatment of the sisters in the Missionaries of Charity. One critic said she wasn't doing anything about the *condition* of the poor as such, but was simply treating *people* that were poor! Many critics, seizing upon her open admissions of the struggle to feel God's closeness during struggle and squalor, even expressed doubts about her faith and sincerity. Her globalism and organizational might were attacked as commercially exploiting her image as a saintly servant when she was actually an aggressive empire-builder for the church. One of the most lasting criticisms against her was the accusation that she was not treating the poor but rather proselytizing souls to the Catholic Church. Of this she offered no apology, saying, "I'm not a social worker. I don't do it for this reason. I do it for Christ. I do it for the church." Finally, always and everywhere, she was vilified the most for her unwavering stance against abortion.

Mother Teresa dealt with such criticism all the days of her public life. She simply refused to live her life for the reasons critics wished to assign her. Not once was she known to recant from her stand on the issues or pull back from her unpopular positions of morality and service. Not everyone agreed with her values, but almost everyone was amazed at her steely spunk. Perhaps no moment is as illustrative of this as her speech given at the National Prayer Breakfast in Washington, D.C., in February 1997. Railing against the practice of abortion, Mother Teresa at one point said, " What is taking place in America is a war against the child. And if we accept that the mother can kill her own child, how can we tell other people not to kill one another?" Conspicuous among the attendees at that prayer breakfast were President and First Lady Bill and Hillary Clinton, politically aligned with the pro-choice side of the abortion question. Undeterred by such prominent figures positioned opposite her politically, Mother Teresa was unafraid and unashamed to state her position defiantly.

This spirit of defiance, of standing for what she believed in no matter who was in opposition, was the same spirit that led her to spearhead a rescue of 37 children trapped in a hospital in a fight between Palestinians and Israelis. It is the same spirit responsible for ministering to the starving masses in Ethiopia, tending to earthquake victims in Albania, and assisting radiation casualties at Chernobyl. It is the strong spirit of a Rascal driven by purpose and living life fully in the service of attacking the status quo. It is the spirit that, at the time of her death in 1997, had produced a charitable service organization of over 4,000 sisters operating over 600 missions in 123 countries with over 100,000 volunteers.

In the words of Nawaz Sharif, Prime Minister of Pakistan, she was a "rare and unique individual who lived long for higher purposes." From the viewpoint of critics and contributors alike, it must be agreed that if anything, Mother Teresa was certainly a Rascal, a title that despite Nobel Peace Prizes and beatification, she likely has not received until now!

CHAPTER 4

The Battle

Rascals are powerful creatures who assault the status quo with a strong sense of purpose and a dream for something better. Their hunger for excellence and passion for significance are what has fueled every great hero story throughout the ages. But nothing worthwhile ever comes easy. There is no victory without a struggle, no overcoming without resistance, and no testimony without a test. The reason for this is Obstaclès. His spiny little head is full of ideas and techniques proven to be effective in thwarting Rascals everywhere.

Obstaclès only looks harmless, but that is by design. It's all about fooling Rascals. In reality, Obstaclès is a deadly and dangerous foe to anyone dreaming of a better life, striving to achieve excellence, and hungering for significance. His arsenal is powerful, his weapons are varied, and he uses them with great skill. However, as Rascals everywhere must discover sooner or later, Obstaclès has no power over us that we don't first give him. Therein lies the battle. Some of the greatest stories ever told come from the clash between Obstaclès and Rascals.

What we have as a result is a classic clash of titans; two forces of magnificent power, poised and determined, squaring off in a romantic battle between good and evil, right and wrong, excellence and decadence. Perhaps Anthony Robbins said it best: "You're in the midst of a war: a battle between the limits of a crowd seeking the surrender of your dreams, and the power of your true vision to create and contribute. It is a fight between those who will tell you what you cannot do, and that part of you that knows / and has always known / that we are more than our environment; and that a dream, backed by an unrelenting will to attain it, is truly a reality with an imminent arrival." E. E. Cummings wrote, "To be nobody but yourself in a world that's doing its best to make you somebody else, is to fight the hardest battle you are ever going to fight. Never stop fighting." These are calls to arms for anyone with even a seed of Rascalinity within. It's a summons to walk toward the sound of the booming guns.

Individual Skirmishes

Every epic war of any size boils down to the individual conflicts raging in the trenches. It is there, in the fierce battle between one opponent directly fighting another, that the spirit of victory or defeat turns the tide and determines final outcomes. It is also there, in the personal fighting, where things get the nastiest. Explosives and guns, bayonets and knives, clubs and gun butts, scratching and biting, and even the throwing of fruit as at the end of the famous naval battle of Lepanto in 1571, are all employed in the frantic effort to kill or be killed.

At the risk of over-dramatizing, the battle for our dreams and the pursuit of significance is just as fierce. And just like in greater physical wars, the battle in the trenches is where our dreams are won or lost.

A Force For Good

I was busy in my home office one morning when my wife Terri walked in with one of my sons, the nine year old. The bottom lip was quivering, anger and frustration were bubbling up, crying had obviously been taking place, and the fight to maintain composure was about to be lost. And that was just Terri! My son didn't look much better, either! Obviously, this was a moment for the wisdom and strength of Dad. The only problem was the complexity of the situation. As it was being explained I tried to keep track of the winding trail of what had happened, looking for motive and things to correct. By the end of the explanation I was as flummoxed as my wife. So much for the wisdom of Dad! What unfolded was an elaborate web of emotional conflict that was not necessarily intentional. It was really just the collateral damage of a young Rascal unsure how to use the powerful Rascal weapons with which he'd been born. He was like a Jedi apprentice with his first light saber, giving it a whirl in a China shop. I said a quick prayer and did my best to "seek first to understand," as recommended by Steven Covey. After my son had completed his nine-year-old style explanation, I quickly attempted to organize the affair in my mind. Finally I was able to piece together about four areas for constructive discussion. Overall, though, I wanted to make an impression that would hit home. I wanted this incident to be a teaching moment through which my young buck could grow. Finally, I lighted upon what he felt to be the key concept. It was simple, really, and it cut through all the emotion and confused jumble of facts.

"What this really comes down to, son," I said, "is the decision of how to use the many gifts you've been given. You are charming, charismatic, persuasive, influential, attractive, funny, athletic, and powerful (taking after his Dad). But what you are going to have to decide is whether you are going to use all that to become a *force for good*, or if you're going to become a selfish jerk like almost everybody else." As we finished the conversation I realized my son's situation had simplified the position in which we all find ourselves. We've all been blessed beyond comprehension. We've all got a list of gifts we've received just as impressive and as powerful as my son's. The key thing, though, is how we are going to deploy them.

Being decadent is easy. Evil is everywhere. It takes nearly nothing to succeed by cheating, lying, stealing, or selling to the profane nature of humanity. Violence, sex, anger, hatred, victimization, and escapism come easy to entertainers and sell easy to a crowd of nobodies. The fastest route to tinsel-town success, the empty kind full of fame and money and no fulfillment, is to sell directly to the clamoring masses the poison for which their blackened hearts crave. The Bible says, "And this is the condemnation, that light is come into the world, and men loved darkness rather than light, because their deeds were evil." Left to our own natures, we love darkness and actually gravitate toward things that aren't good for us. I am never impressed with the angry young faces full of rebellion and hatred on the covers of entertainment magazines. All I see when I look at them is another young person who thinks he is being creative by being bad. It's an old, old story that is neither new nor impressive. There is

> **Left to our own natures, we love darkness and actually gravitate toward things that aren't good for us.**

120

nothing clever or cute about evil. It is playing with fire.

Thomas Mann's classic, *Doctor Faustus*, which draws on a story of older origins, tells the tale of a man selling his soul to the Devil in exchange for fame and fortune as a musical composer. In a hollow way the Devil fulfills his end of the bargain, in that the success in this life that was so dearly purchased is a Hell-on-earth of its own. It destroys the character even before he dies. This *Faustian Bargain* is exactly what results from success obtained the wrong way. Unfortunately, today Mann's drama is being lived by millions.

The best way to describe this choice we all face is by considering the following chart. At the extreme left side is decadence. This is success that is accomplished through courting evil and making

CHOICE OF SUCCESS

Decadence	Excellence
Easier	Harder
Faster	Slower
Unfulfilling	Fulfilling
Destroys Lives	Improves Lives
Temporary Pleasure	Lasting Happiness

a *Faustian Bargain*, by violating what is right in exchange for fame, fortune, and power. This type of success is far quicker and easier than legitimate success that comes from excellence and adding lasting, positive value to people's lives. The problem with this arrangement, though, is that it is not only unfulfilling, but it rots the soul. It is temporary pleasure instead of lasting happiness, has a negative impact on people, and causes destruction of lives. How many stories do we need of young Hollywood starlets checking into rehab, of overnight successes taking their own lives, of broken marriages, overdoses, and police arrests? Such stories are so common they are nearly passé.

At the other end of the spectrum is excellence. This is success accomplished through becoming a *force for good*. It is harder and usually much slower than the decadent kind of success, but it's victory tastes sweet and is fulfilling. It feeds the soul instead of rotting it, leading to happiness. Also, it has a positive impact on the lives of other people and is constructive instead of destructive.

A person told me once he wished his life were as simple as it seemed when he was a child. My reaction was similar to what is being shown here. Life actually is simple if we keep things clearly in mind, if we consider absolute truths for what they really mean. There is a concept called right and wrong. The whole world is not composed entirely of gray areas; there are huge areas of black and white. Our lives grow complicated, messy and hurtful when we lose sight of these simple but powerful truths. Success is the same way. It is a matter of choice. It is a matter of choosing to be a force for good, or not. Real, positive success is actually that simple. It may not be easy, but it is simple.

> **The whole world is not composed entirely of gray areas; there are huge areas of black and white.**

By the way, when we fail to make a choice we still make a choice by not choosing. We may not drift all the way to the left edge of the chart, but we will at least end up somewhere in the middle, where mediocrity and insignificance live. Oddly, though, most people gravitate pretty far toward decadence if not actively choosing to be a force for good. People left to their own nature get sucked into the void where good was supposed to be. This is because evil cannot be defined without first defining 'good.' In fact, we realize that evil is nothing more than the absence of good, just as darkness is not an entity of its own but must be explained by the absence of light.

The word light comes from the Greek word leukos, which means white. Webster defines light in several different ways, including

"Something that makes vision possible," "electromagnetic radiation of any wavelength and traveling in a vacuum with a speed of about 186,281 miles per second," "spiritual illumination," "something that enlightens or informs," "a medium through which light is admitted," "a noteworthy person in a particular place or field," "a particular expression of the eye," "the representation of light in art," and "a flame for lighting something." Note that none of these definitions mentions darkness. Darkness, conversely is defined by Webster as: "devoid or partially devoid of light," "transmitting only a portion of light," and "bearing less light in color than other substances of the same kind." Each of these definitions relies on the readers' foundational understanding of the concept of 'light.' There are other definitions given for darkness, and interestingly, they use the word 'evil,' which itself cannot be defined without the contrast to the word 'good.'

The point is one cannot produce darkness, but can only snuff the light. Likewise, one cannot produce evil; but can only be void of good. Succeeding is not the big issue in our society. There is enough abundance and opportunity for everyone with even basic levels of ambition and drive to make it to some degree. The real issue is which type of success one will pursue. It's up to each of us to decide for ourselves.

It should be apparent by now why it takes a Rascal, as defined in this book, to choose the path of good and significance over evil and decadence: it is a small group heading against the crowd. It involves leaving the comfort of the herd and deciding not to go over the cliff with them. It requires courage of conviction and fortitude over time. The temptation will always be prevalent to default on one's values and change over to the easy path. Rascals, however, finish well.

> **The temptation will always be prevalent to default on one's values and change over to the easy path.**

They stay strong and true to their decision to be a force for good, influencing others in that direction and confounding Obstaclès at every turn. This is why Rascals deserve a hearty salute. They are often unsung heroes in the biggest battle raging in human lives.

The Battle Plan – The Productive Loop

There is a pattern of success for any Rascal choosing to be a force for good and seeking to achieve excellence and significance. It is called the Productive Loop.

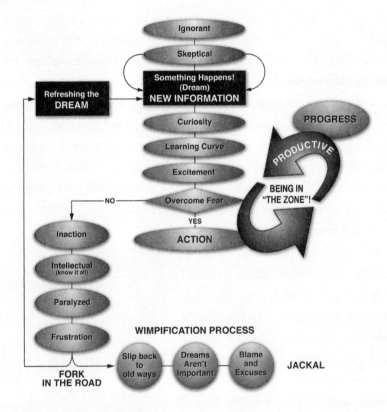

Rascals start out ignorant like everyone else. They simply don't know what they don't know about a certain subject, and they may not even realize they are Rascals. But then new information finds its way into their consciousness, either through a good book, a friend, a life experience, or whatever. This new information suggests a path toward accomplishment, a route of opportunity, an idea to be tried. Immediately, though, upon receiving this new information, most Rascals, being Rascals, are skeptical. They take a mental step back to consider what they are learning with a critical eye. Eventually, however, that new information starts to make sense. This leads to curiosity. The Rascal begins asking 'What if?' questions, considering possibilities. From there the Rascal digs into the learning process. The learning curve is steep because the Rascal is learning quickly, happily gaining knowledge in the direction of this new possibility. Learning becomes extremely fun, because it is so relevant. This leads to excitement. The Rascal can feel the enthusiasm rushing into everything he does. This excitement, in turn, leads to the overcoming of fears. Things that in the past, without this purposeful direction would have held the Rascal back are now no match at all. Small trees are smashed down in front of him, hills are scaled, rivers forded, and mountains climbed as the Rascal is now in hot pursuit of a brighter tomorrow.

This spirited action leads to progress. Progress is one of the best encouragers known to man. Progress builds belief, confidence, and momentum. Progress lets the Rascal know he is on track; his efforts are

> **Progress is one of the best encouragers known to man.**

making an impact, and his learning has merit. Therefore, he learns even more. He applies what he learns, analyzes how it affects his actions, makes adjustments, does more, learns more, and accomplishes more. He is in the Productive Loop. He is in "The Zone".

Life in "The Zone"

"The Zone" is a concept that describes a peak performer in a moment all their own, where they are doing exactly what God built them to do, to the best of their ability, with all of their faculties aligned and intensely focused. It is Michael Jordan in the closing seconds calmly hitting the outside shot to win the game. It is Peyton Manning in the final two minutes marching a team to victory. It is Winston Churchill in "Britain's finest hour," standing defiantly in the bombed-out streets of London waving the two-fingered sign for victory. It is your child getting all A's and giving her Valedictorian speech. It is the lion crouching poised in the grass focusing on a Gazelle. It is those moments when a champion gets to call on all the hours of preparation, planning, and practice and put it all together. It is a rare, true moment in life. It is when one's actions are perfectly in line with one's purpose. Being in The Zone is one of life's most rewarding, fulfilling, memorable moments. It's a natural euphoria. It's living life in a most alive way. Champions, once getting a taste of life lived in such a way, strive to get back into The Zone as often as possible. In essence, The Zone is where Rascals live. They love it there.

The impact a Rascal makes in The Zone is nothing short of incredible. Watching top athletes, for instance, one can sense that they are simply but amazingly going to find a way to win against impossible odds. That's what makes performances in The Zone so remarkable. They represent thousands of hours in preparation of mastery culminating in one moment. It is the ripened fruit of a long and careful planting. It is so powerful that it captures our attention and draws our applause.

Most of us, however, will not become professional athletes. In no way does this diminish either the possibility or the importance of living in The Zone. Anyone in any endeavor can and should seek to find his way to this peak level of performance. Business

126

men and women, surgeons, painters, engineers, preachers, contractors, charity workers, etc., should all find a way to follow the principles represented by a top athlete at the pinnacle of his game and apply it to their calling. The Bible says, "Whether therefore ye eat, or drink, or *whatsoever ye do*, do all to the glory of God."

Those in my audiences who *don't* understand what I am talking about can barely even relate to a Rascal. They don't speak the same language, feel the same impulses, or have the same magnitude of dreams and aspirations. They don't live in The Zone. Instead, *ME!* they live *zoned out*, and it's a shame. They don't know what they are missing. That is why I speak and write upon this topic; to invite people into The Zone. Everyone is invited, but only Rascals respond. The great news, though, is that nobody gets to choose for *CHOOSE* you. It's all up to you. Anyone can choose to do what it takes to be *BEING THE* a Rascal and perform to such a peak as to find himself in The Zone. *KEYWORD!*

Don't think that Obstaclès isn't actively at work trying to stop Rascals everywhere from succeeding as a force for good. He is poised and ready at every step of their journey to throw up barriers and dig potholes. Obstaclès particularly hates it when Rascals are in The Zone, because he knows that in those moments his weapons have the least effect. As the old saying goes, "A dog in the hunt doesn't know it has fleas." Rascals are not bothered by Obstaclès' tactics when they are in The Zone, focused and entirely committed to their task.

The Wimpification Process

Sometimes, however, Obstaclès succeeds in coaxing a Rascal out of The Zone. It could be any of his weapons that do the trick, from fear to distraction to low self-confidence to a failure in character, relationship challenges, or any of the others. The net result is the same: where once the Rascal was overcoming fears and learning and doing with excitement and enthusiasm, now the Rascal caves in to fears and falls into inaction.

Inaction is an especially dangerous condition for a Rascal. Armies are powerful and useful during war but extremely dangerous when idle. A ship may be safe in the harbor but it was not made for the harbor. Similarly, a Rascal may find himself idle but he was not made to be idle. It has been said that, "Idle hands are the Devil's workshop," and this is very true for a mighty Rascal who has suddenly spun out of the Productive Loop. Immediately the Rascal begins to think and analyze and falls into "analysis paralysis." He starts questioning his once-held beliefs, wondering about this and doubting about that. The less action he puts forth the more his mind intellectualizes, becoming like some elite thinker that never accomplishes anything. The Rascal begins to think he knows everything even though he is doing nothing. The natural result of this is a loss of confidence in self and in the cause for which the Rascal had once fought so valiantly. This leads to paralysis as fear sets in even further. When there is no overcoming of fear through action, there is instead an amplification of fear through focusing on it.

Paralysis then leads to frustration. The Rascal starts looking at his or her lack of results. A negative perspective takes over and what used to be inspiring now becomes mocking. Obstaclès begins hurling his taunts, "See? I told you it was a waste of your time," and "Look at all that work you put in and you've still got nothing to show for it," and "Maybe someone else could do it, but *you* certainly can't," or the more blatant, "You're not good enough."

Frustration is the moment of truth, of peak danger, a fork in the road. It is at moments of peak frustration where many Rascals leave the path of excellence never to return. This is where Rascal "wanna-be's" turn into Rascal "has-beens." It doesn't necessarily even happen dramatically or all at once. It is usually gradual. At first the Rascal just backs off from the learning and associating with other Rascals. He puts down the good books and stops focusing on his goals and dreams. Then he starts slipping back into his old ways, embracing the old vices and convincing himself that it really isn't so bad. Everyone is tempted by ease and familiar comforts, and there is a relief that surges in when a Rascal first takes the pressure off himself. He mistakes this temporary feeling of release for vindication of his choice at the fork in the road. Most people are slow to admit to themselves that they've taken the destructive path at the fork. They fake themselves out that they are "still a Rascal" and are "still going to do it," it's just that they are "going to take a little time off," "back off a little bit," "work on themselves a little," "get through this season or situation," "finish re-evaluating," etc. The specific excuses don't matter because no one believes them anyway; certainly not other Rascals who can see quitting for what it is, and the quitter doesn't really believe the excuses either. The excuses are just sufficient to pacify the quitter long enough to allow him to slide further down the slippery slope of mediocrity.

Through this whole "Wimpification Process," Obstaclès is at his worst. He understands how to build momentum in a downward direction. So next he goes to work convincing the Rascal has-been that his dreams weren't that important anyway. "The cause wasn't that important, either," he reminds, them. "Things are okay as they are. There is no use wasting one's life pursuing ideals and trying to make a difference. Doesn't this new life of ease feel good after expending so much effort toward the silly concept of being excellent and living for significance? Who needs life in The Zone anyway, that's just for fanatics. And making a difference? Who were you kidding? The problems in this world are too big for one person to do anything about. You might as well just kick back and enjoy your life instead of wasting it by pounding against immovable objects. Be-

> **Losers must always provide an excuse for their lack of winning.**

sides, you only live once, best to live it up before it's too late."

The final steps are justification and blame. Losers must always provide an excuse for their lack of winning. This begins with justification. It is a search for an excuse plausible enough to hide behind, first for the quitter, then for everyone he'll tell. This justification rarely involves any responsibility on the part of the has-been Rascal. It is always someone else's fault, or at the very least, it's a situation that's to blame. As the great Austrian psychiatrist Alfred Adler wrote, "The life-lie of the neurotic: it is a categorical demand of the patient's life plan that he or she should fail through the guilt of others and thus be free from any responsibility." People will justify almost anything to themselves, when it serves their cowardice and covers their failures. Justification is the door through which character departs.

Justification is the door through which character departs.

Now these could-have-beens reach the bottom: blame. The facts don't count because the top priority at this stage of the game is justifying quitting and hanging the reasons for it on someone or something else. *Someone* is to blame, and since it can't be the quitter it must reside elsewhere. The search is on for a scapegoat and nearly anything or anyone will suffice. Be careful dealing with people when they are at this point because nearly anything you say or do will get chosen as the reason for their ineptitude and failure. You will become the convenient reason for their Wimpification.

There is a name for people who were once on the path to becoming an official Rascal, but instead succumb to the slippery slope of the Wimpification Process and scorn Rascals and the principles for which they stand: Jackals. These are the people who not only waste their talents and individuality by settling for a life of ease and mediocrity, but give in to the lures of Obstaclès and unwittingly join his minions. Jackals don't just choose an easier path for themselves, they throw stones at those who would dare take the high road of excellence and achievement. Jackals become the natural enemy of Rascals everywhere because a Rascal's example eliminates a Jackal's excuses. The higher the courage of a Rascal, the more the cowardice of a Jackal comes to light. The bigger the Rascal's accomplishment, the more obvious the Jackal's failure. Although this condition doesn't have to be permanent, sadly, it often is.

Jackals can never be fatal to a Rascal's purpose, but like thorns on the high plains, they can be a constant annoyance and a temporary source of pain. When encountering Jackals, Rascals should take note that without diligence, they could share the same fate: a cynical and wasted life.

In the end, the choice between staying the Rascal course or succumbing to the temptations of Wimpification come down to this: Rascals hate losing enough to change while those who Wimpify hate changing enough to lose.

Revisiting the Fork in the Road

This is a dismal crash analysis, to be sure. But it doesn't have to end this way. Let's go back to the fork in the road where it all went wrong to see that even when things appear their darkest, a true Rascal still has a choice. Remember that the Wimpification process was caused by inaction, over-intellectualizing, analysis paralysis, and peak frustration. That is what brought the Rascal to the fork in the road. But by definition a fork has two options. It's the *other* option chosen by the Rascal that makes all the difference. Understand: there is no shame in getting frustrated, falling into inaction, or having doubts and discouragements. It happens to everybody. Champions, however, keep these moments to a minimum and always find a way to pull out of them. How do they do this? By taking the other side of that fork in the road.

This sounds simple but it is not easy. The choice takes energy, but it has to be made at a time when energy and belief are likely at their lowest. But simply understanding this diagram as a way to see through Obstaclès' tricks should be helpful. A Rascal realizes what is happening to him and realizes that even at the point of peak frustration he *still* retains the personal freedom of *choosing*. Victor Frankl wrote, "everything can be taken from a man but one thing: the last of his freedoms - to choose one's attitude in any given set of circumstances, to choose one's own way."

> "Everything can be taken from a man but one thing: the last of his freedoms - to choose one's attitude in any given set of circumstances, to choose one's own way."
> - Victor Frankl

At this moment we see the courage of the Rascal tested to the limit. Making the choice against momentum and Obstaclès to fight one's way back into the Productive Loop will require a deep, meaningful reason. It is here that the three levels of motivation play such an important part - particularly, the deepest reasons of cause, purpose, significance and leaving a legacy. Reasons with the depth and importance of these will most likely be necessary for the Rascal to make a courageous choice. Without a big cause there is no big hero. Rascals realize at this critical moment that anything valuable and worthwhile requires the paying of a price. They un-

132

derstand that the bigger the commitment, the bigger the contribution, the greater the reward. They remember why they started out in the first place and refresh those dreams and causes in their minds until they reconnect with them emotionally. They stoke the tiny flame of the pilot light still burning within them and feed it fuel. Rascals encourage themselves by remembering that the worse the odds and the bigger the opposition, the better the drama and the more fascinating the story. In short, Rascals remember their dream.

Having made the choice not to Wimpify, a Rascal seeks the association of other Rascals within whose company he can be strengthened and rebuilt. He refreshes his dreams and gets acquainted with the details of his cause again. He goes back to the basic reasons he began this journey in the first place. He plugs back in to the learning cycle and starts to gain new information about the fundamentals of what he does while learning new techniques and methods that can improve his performance over what he did before. This new information leads to renewed excitement and the overcoming of fears. Then, action steps invigorate him and he feels his old strength returning. The more action he takes the more progress he sees as evidence that he's made a wise and courageous choice. This progress fuels further learning and the Rascal has chosen himself back into the Productive Loop. Taken far enough with enough commitment, his renewed vigor might even lead him back into the highest level of the Productive Loop, that wonderful place called The Zone.

At this point, the Rascal is back! Obstaclès is forced back to the drawing board in frustration, planning his next attack with renewed hatred. And so the cycle goes throughout the life of a Rascal. Always tempted, always maligned, a Rascal knows his path is fraught with danger. He is a Rascal, though, because he presses forward boldly.

Rascals wage their individual battles against Obstaclès gallantly, knowing that their fight *in the trenches* has a tremendous impact on the overall battle raging in society. Rascals know that one person can and does make a difference, and strive mightily to do their part. This will involve criticism and resistance, and may even result in the opposition throwing fruit! Undeterred, Rascals become a force for good and attack the status quo, striving to leave things better than they found them.

John Wycliffe

John Wycliffe was a fourteenth century Oxford scholar. Charismatic, fluent in Latin, and a major philosopher and theologian, Wycliffe was living the life of a sequestered intellectual professor. He was well respected and ensconced in the halls of academia. For most, that would have been the end of the story; but not for Wycliffe.

It was a time of unbelievable church dominance, in which the church was a government all its own, crossing national and/ or feudal borders and commanding control over every aspect of people's lives. It was powerful, often suppressive, political, bureaucratic, and sometimes ruthless. It had a monopoly on worship in most of Europe, and controlled church attendance, taxation, private behavior, and even sex. The prevailing attitude was that the church was the guardian and interpreter of all Scripture, and the common people had no right to their own understanding of God's truths apart from the pronouncements of the official church. From our vantage point nearly seven hundred years later, it is difficult to imagine. Nothing exists in today's world to resemble it.

It was real enough for Wycliffe, however, and he felt driven to do something about it. According to author Melvyn Bragg, "His prime revolutionary argument, one which, if accepted in any shape or form, would have toppled the Church entirely, was that the Bible was the sole authority for religious faith and practice and that everyone had the right to read and interpret scripture for himself. This would have changed the world, and those who ruled the world knew it. He was to become their prime enemy." Wycliffe decided to square off against this gargantuan power by an act that today sounds so harmless; providing a Bible translated into the common language of the English people. To that point it had only been available in Latin, which none but priests could understand. Wycliffe was convinced that getting the truth to the people by placing the Scriptures in their own hands and in their own language was worth risking his very life.

The translation itself was a huge task, but producing and disseminating the final copies was even more difficult, as everything had to be done in secret. Hidden production lines were established, and hundreds of volunteers rose up to help in the clandestine movement. Wycliffe then trained itinerant preachers to get the books to the people and teach them the Scriptures, which they could now verify by their own readings. They became known as the Lollards, a word taken from the root meaning "to mumble." Calling themselves the Christian Brethren, their movement spread high and low throughout England and Scotland, with thousands of copies of the Wycliffe English Bible permeating the countryside.

The church began by officially condemning Wycliffe. They complained that "the jewel of the clerics is turned to the sport of the laity and the pearl of the gospel is scattered abroad and trodden underfoot by swine." In 1382, a synod of the church declared Wycliffe and his followers to be heretics. They were soon gathered up, tortured, and killed. English Bibles were confiscated and burned. Later, the English Parliament enacted a ban on all English language Bibles. Bragg wrote, "After Wycliffe's death and despite the condemnation and harshness of the Church, copies of Wycliffe's Bible continued to be produced and circulated - even when it became a mortal crime to own any of Wycliffe's works. With astonishing courage, Catholics who spread the English language were prepared to defy the Pope and take a chance with their lives and their eternal souls in order to read the word of God to the English in their own language." As is common with extreme Rascals such as Wycliffe, the work lived on.

Though Wycliffe's efforts were largely snuffed, the seeds had been planted. Where Wycliffe and his Lollards had been stopped, William Tyndale and others would later succeed. Within a little over a century, the same English government that had been so zealous in helping the church eliminate any and all English Bibles would officially sponsor the publication of one of the most famous Bibles in history; the King James. Wycliffe had not fought in vain.

CHAPTER 5

The Cause

What Will You Do Without Freedom?

The battle in the trenches each Rascal faces as he strives to be a force for good with excellence and significance is part of a larger global picture. There is a bigger war. So as a Rascal slugs it out one-on-one with Obstaclès for his own individual victory, his personal gains are not the only ones at stake, and he can take stock in the fact that he doesn't fight alone. Other Rascals are swinging away right beside him on the parapet. Also, every Rascal needs to understand that his or her efforts toward individual success contribute to the overall war, and sometimes in ways that have massive ramifications.

Joshua Lawrence Chamberlain, a college professor, was awarded the Congressional Medal of Honor for his conduct at the Battle of Gettysburg. In command of the 20th Maine at the far left flank of the Union line, he found himself at the pivot point of the entire battle. Realizing the importance of not allowing the confederates to turn his flank, Chamberlain and his men fought stubbornly atop their little hill. Nearly out of ammunition and facing yet another charge from the tough 15th Alabama regiment, Chamberlain ordered his men to affix their bayonets and charge down the hill into their attackers. He conducted a 'swinging gate' charge which flanked the Alabamians and captured many. It was a brave and daring act that had a massive effect on the overall battle. The result was that the Union army held onto its advantageous high ground position. The next day General Lee ordered the ill-fated "Picket's Charge" which many call the "High Water Mark" of the Confederacy; never again would the South be in the ascendancy. The war had turned. This example is a clear and dramatic picture of the conflict in the trenches impacting the overall war.

There is an old philosophy that says if every man protects his family by staying safely ensconced in the comfort of his own home until the barbarians find their way to his door, he will lose all. However, if each man will volunteer to leave his own cozy cottage and make his way to the city walls, together he and the rest of the town can repel the invaders. This is how fighting for purpose and cause and meaning plays out. It can't be done in a vacuum, it is *not only* about one individual Rascal's success. Rascals everywhere need to know they must band together to preserve the very conditions that allow them to be Rascals in the first place. There must be an environment in which each Rascal is free to choose his rebel path, to pursue his courageous goals, and to accomplish his crazy dreams. That environment must be protected. Without that environment of freedom there can be no Rascals. In the larger scheme of things, that's what a Rascal's individual efforts contribute towards; freedom and justice for all.

A Rascal cannot logically learn all the principles we've covered to this point in this book about *individual success* and not believe in the *larger principles* of *freedom and justice for all*. He cannot pile up his own accomplishments selfishly within his own life while the freedom that allowed his success is attacked at the city walls. He also can't use his freedom to achieve great things and then attack the very structures that provided him the opportunities in the first place.

Sadly, though, many would-be Rascals behave this way. They understand the Productive Loop and they defy Obstacles on a regular basis, but they don't understand the ramifications of the larger picture and they don't align themselves with the forces fighting for good on a global scale. Instead, they become elitist in their thinking and do things that undermine the very foundations upon which they stand. Without an environment of freedom, most of the concepts for taking advantage of opportunities in one's life are not even relevant. Without freedom there is no opportunity. To quote *Braveheart's* William Wallace once again, "What will you do without freedom?" The answer is, "not much."

Give Me Liberty or Give Me Death

"Give me liberty or give me death," are the famous words of Patrick Henry that used to be taught to every school child. A handful of American patriots took those words seriously, and so have countless others through the years. Their actions are proof enough of the value of freedom.

Pavel Ivanovich Dudnikov was captain of the Soviet fishing trawler *Vishera*. Ten years before, he had obtained some Western currency in the hope of trading in foreign goods to supplement his meager government-controlled income and feed his family. He was caught by government authorities and sentenced to eight years in a labor camp. In 1972 he risked capture by patrol boats and defied the informer aboard his own ship. He sailed from his home port of Kerch all the way across the Black Sea, through the Bosporus and the Sea of Marmara, through the Aegean, and into the port of Piraeus near Athens, Greece. It was the first Soviet vessel to successfully defect since the end of World War II. Dudnikov was free.

Peter Dobler had been preparing for a long time with endurance swims in cold rivers at night and working to condition his body during the day. He mapped his route meticulously and studied every nautical chart at his disposal, learning dead-reckoning and celestial navigation techniques. Finally conditions were right and on July 23, 1971 he swam away from the East German resort beach in Kuhlungsborn straight out into the cold Baltic Sea. Evading search lights from the coast and East German patrol boats that came within yards of him, Dobler swam over 28 miles to cross the Baltic and make his way into West German territory. In the water for over 26 hours, Dobler was picked up by West German pleasure boaters and carried into freedom.

Eufemio Delgado hated living in Communist Cuba and three times had spoken out against the regime, only to be arrested by the G-2 police each time on 'suspicion of counterrevolutionary activity.' "Is it a crime to say that people don't have enough food?" he asked stubbornly. A truck driver, Delgado returned from a trip one day and his wife told him, "If you have ever heard a child cry from hunger, it is something you never want to hear again." "That does it!" Delgado, father of four, shouted in reply. "We've *got* to get out of this place." 130 people agreed with Delgado and were loaded into his truck. Carefully, Delgado picked his exit point carefully, then crashed his rig through the ditch and fencing separating Communist Cuba from the free American military base in Guantanamo. The truck ground to a halt before making it all the way through and the people poured out of the back and ran for it, climbing over barbed wire fence and concrete barriers while machine gun bullets tore into them. United States marines arrived on the other side and rescued 88 men, women, and children, but sadly, more than 40 others had not made it. Delgado had engineered the single biggest escape from Communist Cuba to that point. They were free.

Alfred Lauterbach was an artist who had seen his brother tortured to death by Soviet soldiers. Thereafter he joined the underground resistance movement. Captured, he was sentenced to 25 years in prison for crimes of conspiracy against the state. He was sent to the infamous Brandenburg Penitentiary in East Germany from which no one had ever escaped. "I was branded as a criminal because I fought against crime," he said. Asked to paint Communist propaganda posters in his prison cell, Lauterbach impressed Horst Bock, his young guard who was in charge of the project. Forming a friendship, the men realized that by being citizens of East Germany they were both, in fact, prisoners. Their moment came when they were authorized to sell a stack of old newspapers to earn money to cover a book-keeping mistake at the prison. With Bock driving and Lauterbach hiding beneath a stack of papers, the two men drove from the prison to the Havel River, where they swam right past patrol boats and into freedom.

Armando Socarras Ramirez was only seventeen years old but had already grown tired of Communist Cuba. He lived with eleven other people in one room, his food was rationed and scarce, and he had no choice over his life's occupation. He and a friend huddled in the weeds at the end of the runway at Jose Marti airport in Havana and waited for the DC-8 Flight 904 to turn and stop before making its takeoff for Madrid, Spain. At that moment they scampered onto the runway and climbed up the landing gear into the chamber above it. Nearly crushed as the gear came up into position upon takeoff, Ramirez somehow managed to avoid being burned by the hot tires and hung on tightly to a pipe. His friend fell out and was arrested. The overnight, 5,563 mile, 8 hour and 20 minute flight would climb to 29,000 feet and see temperatures as low as -41 degrees F. Ramirez should have been crushed and burned by the landing gear. He should have frozen to death in the extreme temperatures and low pressurization. But somehow he survived and found freedom. "Even knowing the risks," he said, "I would try to escape again if I had to."

Pavel Ivanovich Dudnikov, Peter Dobler, Eufemio Delgado, Alfred Lauterbach, Horst Bock, and Armando Socarras Ramirez were all Rascals that understood freedom. They understood it most clearly because they didn't have it. Communism and Socialism and Statism and Collectivism weren't philosophical concepts to them - they were *real*. And to escape the tyrannies that always accompany those "isms", these brave Rascals risked everything. "Give me liberty or give me death," indeed.

Freedom Under Attack

Freedom is precious and rare, but freedom isn't free, and it never has been. In the moments and places freedom has flourished on the earth, it was purchased dearly by Rascals who stood up to tyranny and sacrificed so others might go free. Freedom is *so dear* Rascals everywhere have been willing to risk *everything* to gain it.

Encouraging free people to notice and appreciate their freedom is like telling a fish about water. When it's all you've ever known and you're literally submerged in it, you tend to take it for granted. But just as a fish tank can be drained, so can freedom. When freedom is lost, it always looks the same. You can pick any time in history in any location where freedom was lost and what you will find is the oppression of the many by a few. Justice dies and the liberties of innocent people are obliterated. Families are destroyed. Property is confiscated. Suffering becomes the norm. Innocent people die like crops in a drought. Despair is pervasive. Poverty is followed by malnutrition and disease. Technology and the arts slow to a crawl as the vast majority of the people are caught in a death grip of daily survival.

Where are the Rascals at such times? Most of them are murdered in their prime to eliminate them as a threat to the power in charge. This is because tyrants know true Rascals are their greatest enemy. Rascals know the truth about freedom and they fight tirelessly to protect it, and that's what makes them dangerous.

> **Rascals know the truth about freedom and they fight tirelessly to protect it, and that's what makes them dangerous.**

Freedom is under attack in our times. Only this battle is not a military one, rather, it's an ideological one. It's being fought for in the minds and hearts of the people. Rascals everywhere need to be aware of it. There is a war raging across our lands and the stakes are high. It's an all-or-nothing slug-fest. Ideas have consequences, and poor ideas such as Communism and Socialism have extremely *dire* consequences. The stories of the valiant escapes that we just considered only happen when people are oppressed and their freedoms are taken away. If machine guns and fences and patrol boats are required to force a population to "enjoy the benefits" of the government and its philosophy, it's a pretty good bet that the philosophy stinks. Freedom needs no fences.

A Freedom Education and a Leadership Revolution

The war being waged for freedom follows the same lines as it always has; power wielded by those using it to oppress others. This has always been done by force, fear, money, governments, armies, and control of all forms. Wherever control can be gained, it will get used. Whenever an inch of authority over someone is given, a yard will be taken. As soon as the door is cracked open even a smidgeon, it will eventually be wrenched open and yanked off its hinges.

> The war being waged for freedom follows the same lines as it always has; power wielded by those using it to oppress others.

It's a lot like allowing a camel to poke his nose under the tent flap. Just let him in a little, and before you know it he has used his strength and stubbornness to force his way in completely; his big, flea-bitten body filling the whole tent. It's the same with tyranny. Government programs and control start small at first, promising to remain small or even temporary. But as Ronald Reagan once quipped, "There is nothing quite so permanent as a temporary government program."

145

This is why the American governmental experiment, as created in the Constitution of the United States, is such a rare and precious thing. In its founding principles are a structure and a concept of establishing a government *for* the people and not *over* the people. It was established primarily to limit and divide the powers of government from bracket-creep and control. In most governments on the planet today and throughout history, the people have existed to serve the state. But in the minds of the founding fathers of the United States, a government was instituted *to serve the people*, and to govern *by their consent*. Oliver DeMille wrote, "It is, after all, what the [American] Revolution was about: either live to work for aristocrats or live to build for oneself and one's posterity."

It was a radical idea. So radical, in fact, that it shook the foundations of monarchies and dictatorships around the world and ushered in an era of revolutions and freedom. In many places these revolutions succeeded, but often, as in the case of the French Revolution, the principles were not the same and the rebellion led to even worse tyranny than before. The lesson of the French Revolution was that the principles upon which a revolution and/or government are founded matter - they *really* matter! Western civilization hit a new plateau as more and more government structures sought to model at least some of the principles of the United States. The closer they came to a government *of the people* and not *over the people*, the freer they were and the longer they lasted.

It is imperative to understand this concept that principles and ideas matter. The consequences are enormous. This is one reason why Rascals are so important; they don't swallow ideas and ideologies blindly, they think for themselves and make up their own minds. Nobody can program or indoctrinate them into any "politically correct" way of

> "If a nation expects to be ignorant and free, it expects what never was and never will be."
> - Thomas Jefferson

thinking. They are free and independent mavericks, unwilling to "heil" any Hitler. In fact, a population comprised of such a rabble is one of the freest and safest possible. As Thomas Jefferson so accurately stated, "If a nation expects to be ignorant and free, it expects what never was and never will be." Hans Schmitt was raised in Nazi Germany. He wrote, "Germany has taught me that an uncritical view of the national past generated an equally subservient acceptance of the present."

The biggest weapon a Rascal has against the encroachment upon his freedoms is education and awareness. In a broader sense, a population adequately packed with such Rascals is the key to the long-term preservation of freedom. Oliver DeMille, in his excellent book, *The Coming Aristocracy*, wrote:

> "What is needed is for 'regular' people - citizens from the middle and lower classes - to attain the education of mid- and long-term, by doing what the upper classes have always done and still do: obtain great, mentored education . . . . Leadership Education never died. The elites have used is as the key to maintaining their power. In the Information Age, educational quality (defined as the level of one's ability and tendency to think - broadly, deeply, on any new topic, and effectively across all time spans) is the greatest determining factor of prosperity and freedom. The solution is Leadership Education for everyone! The future of freedom depends on it."

To preserve freedom, Rascals need to be educated on what is really going on. This is because a fundamental failing in understanding will result in wrong conclusions.

> **To preserve freedom, Rascals need to be educated on what is really going on.**

Therefore, Rascals need to interpret any information and indoctrination critically (including this book). They need to be awake to the forces swirling around them. They need what DeMille calls a Leadership Education. In our book *Launching a Leadership Revolution*, Orrin Woodward and I listed *learning* as the first, primary level of influence in a leader's journey. This was to prepare and continue to inform a leader's actions as he launched himself on a journey of striving to make a difference, influencing his own behavior so he could gain greater influence with those around him. The exponential power of a positive revolution in leadership begins where individuals take initiative and responsibility right where they are, in what they are doing, with what they have at their disposal, each working to make the world a better place. This happens, as we saw with Lawrence Chamberlain at the Battle of Gettysburg, as one leader's actions affects the larger picture in an outward ripple effect of influence, spreading like the disturbance in calm water from the hurling of a pebble. In this way one person, one leader, one Rascal, can and does make a difference. But it all starts with an education about freedom. Freedom depends on a bunch of Rascals knowing what is actually going on.

Participation, Involvement and Finances

Being informed and growing in leadership and influence are maximized when the Rascal is involved in his local government, participates in community affairs, and plays a part in his civic world. Too many of us allow busy lives, financial challenges, apathy, and feelings of insignificance hold us back from participation. One thing is for sure: the special interest groups, recipients of government hand-outs, corporations with special deals,

> "The only thing necessary for the triumph of evil is for good men to do nothing."
> - Edmund Burke

and power-brokers eager to enact their own agendas, will all be extremely active in public affairs, whether overtly or secretly. Rascals should be at least as active in opposition. In the famous words of Irish politician Edmund Burke: "The only thing necessary for the triumph of evil is for good men to do nothing." Rascals are never aloof, they engage.

Money and power have always been related. Some have used money to gain power; others power to gain money. Many have been consumed by both. Whatever the case, it is an unfortunate fact that those without financial ability are therefore at least somewhat limited in their scope and reach. This shouldn't discourage Rascals with limited financial means from doing their best to exert influence for good on the world around them. After all, we have clearly seen the power of a Rascal's behavior through the examples of Mother Teresa, Andre de Jong, and others who had little or no money when beginning their efforts. However, the bold truth is that good people with financial power often have much more influence than if they were less endowed.

What this means for Rascals everywhere is that they should be awake to the need for financial education. It is not acceptable for a Rascal bent on making a difference to be ignorant of finances and the principles of wealth. Misconceptions, misunderstandings, and deliberate complication of financial issues by the governing elites are not allowable for an influential Rascal. For this reason, Rascals should launch themselves on their own program of financial education; learning all they can about the principles of personal financial success. As with all learning, Rascals should not simply stop at education, but shoot for applying this knowledge toward growing their own financial standing. More money means more influence, more funds available for good causes, and an extended reach. The world is full of good ideas, intentions, and programs, but more often than not what is lacking is funding. Rascals empowered by finances are a significant threat to the status quo.

149

Ideas at War - Obstaclès' World View vs. The Rascal World View

All the complicated philosophies of intellectuals down through the ages have accumulated into a handful of overall mindsets. Francis Shaeffer called these collective mindsets *world views.* In his description, a world view represents the lens through which we see the world around us. It involves how we perceive truth, what we think of life's ultimate questions, the principles in which we believe, our faith life, and any other major contributors to how life is perceived and interpreted by our minds. Obviously, there are as many world views as there are people, no two people being exactly a like. However, through the complicated jumble of theories and postulates, all of these world views can be clumped together and simplified into a handful of major groups. Even these can be further combined until two very dominant and opposing world views can clearly be seen among people living in what used to be called 'western civilization.' In fact, western civilization got to be classified as a civilization chiefly because its populations shared a dominant world view and subscribed to mostly shared major principles together. The fruits of this world view, though not all perfect and without challenges and sins, have been incredible. Free nations, the Industrial Revolution, a Republican Democracy, the Information Age and an explosion of masterpieces in music, painting, architecture, sculpture and drama were just some of the products. It is safe to say that some of the most productive, creative, and beautiful works of human hands and minds resulted from the fruits of the constructs of western civilization.

In that same period, however, wars escalated from local tribal affairs into world-wide conflagrations. Murder and killing went from battlefields and individual man's sins to state-sponsored genocides, the magnitude of which the world had never seen. Somehow out of the same civilization that produced a Bach and a Michelangelo came Hitler and Stalin.

This is why it is so critical for Rascals to be educated. Their talents are needed in a revolution that knows who the enemy is, recognizes dangerous ideas for what they are, and meets them at the city gates in fierce opposition.

In the following chart can be seen a compilation of the two major opposing world views at work in our society today. Although no such generalization is totally accurate, and nobody believes in any combination of ideas the exact same way, this chart is still helpful as a map is for proper navigation. It is meant to clearly delineate the battle lines for the future of freedom and western civilization.

Obstacles World View vs	Rascal World View
Control	Freedom
Big government	Big Individual
Relativism	Absolutes
Indoctrination	Education
Rights	Responsibility
Entitlement	Merit
Equal Results	Equal Opportunity
Accolades and "Bonafides"	Accomplishment
Aristocracy	Meritocracy
Perfection of Man	Sinful Man
Laws to Empower the State	Laws to Protect the Individual
World Government	Limited National Governments
Fiat Money Systems	Sound Money Systems
Groups	Individuals
Science as God	Science of God
Economic Controls	Free Markets

Man on the Throne	God on the Throne
Worship of Creation	Worship of Creator
Government Over the People	Government For the People
Legislated Welfare State	Individual Compassion

Again, while each of these categories is a generalization, they should serve to illustrate the concepts that Obstaclès uses to bring his ideas to fruition. As with most ideas, implemented in a level of moderation, they may be perfectly fruitful and legitimate. The problem occurs when ideas get advanced further and further in their implementation. And, as they interact with other ideas in Obstaclès' arsenal, they combine to become even worse for the cause of freedom. There is a trap in most of the categories comprising Obstaclès' World View, however. Obstaclès can make each one sound good, stemming from compassion and appealing to the guilt or generosity of his listeners. He is also famous for fanning the flames of hatred, envy, greed and distinction in order to win converts to his way of thinking. While some of these can be made to sound decent and good, it is really like playing with fire. It's warming and attractive until it burns; then it's too late.

To be fair, many of the ideas in the Rascal World View have been incorrectly implemented in the past or misused and/or abused also. Remember, it's a fallen world, and there are no perfect solutions that are going to come from the hands of man. Also, please shy away from the oversimplification politician's like to draw concerning "right" and "left." The above comparisons do not fit so neatly into such labels and should not be construed to do so. I believe in freedom and the rights of the individual, no matter which way the political parties and their winds happen to blow. I am not wedded to labels and parties but to principles.

The main thing to understand is the more a Rascal's World View is implemented, the more general freedom results. Conversely, the more the Obstaclès World View is implemented, the less freedom results. This is because the ideas represented by the Rascal view lead to individuals having more choices. Whereas the ideas represented by the Obstaclès side limit the choices of individuals. As Bob McEwen teaches, politics is a battle among people to determine where a country will exist on the continuum between the two dominant viewpoints. People will either have more choices and more freedom OR less choices and less freedom. It's as simple as that.

> "Once you understand, you will care!"
> - Bob McEwen

At this point, some people might tune out because they think they don't care about any of this. But one more Bob McEwen quote is warranted: "Once you understand, you will care!"

It is beyond the scope of this book to delve into each of the categories of ideas represented in this chart, rather, this discussion is just to inspire some thought and point out where the battle lines are drawn. Rascals will seek their own education and dig into these topics to learn more about freedom and how to defend it, and as always, make their own decisions. As with any learning, the more one learns, the more he or she wants to learn. With a freedom education, because it matters so much, this is doubly true. Some of the most rewarding time a Rascal will ever spend is in learning about these great ideas and drawing his or her own conclusions. Rascals, after all, can do no less.

Interestingly and tragically, the Obstaclès World View has been tried many times. It is not new theory crying out for an experimental attempt. It is not a worthy ideology looking to prove itself - quite the contrary. For whatever reason, many places and times have given the Obstaclès World View fair hearing. Governments and societies have been founded based upon its principles (almost always forcefully and with bloody hands). It is not new, it is not modern, it is not progressive or enlightened; it is the same old failure dressed up in different terminology. It is oppression of the weak and innocent at the hands of the strong and dominant. It is man thinking he is so smart he can out-fox human nature. And it has *never* worked. It has resulted in the genocides of the twentieth century and the barbed-wire fences, patrol boats and search lights from which Pavel Ivanovich Dudnikov, Peter Dobler, Eufemio Delgado, Alfred Lauterbach, Horst Bock, and Armando Socarras Ramirez all found it necessary to escape.

What is absolutely perplexing to Rascals everywhere, then, is the continued adherence to the ideas of the Obstaclès World View by people who should be smart enough to know better. One is left to conclude that they are either extremely ignorant of their history, or understand it perfectly well and are happy enough to wish to be among the elite that oppresses the rest. As the masses in the middle are unthinkingly swayed by the rhetoric and angry passions stirred up by Obstaclès and his world view, Rascals everywhere shudder. They know the truth of the saying by George Santayana, "Those who do not remember the past are condemned to repeat it."

The Blue Pill or the Red Pill

The epic battle illuminated by the opposing world views of Obstaclès and Rascals is one thing that separates a Rascal from a hoodlum. Many traits of a Rascal are dangerous and could be found among pirates, vagabonds, and any other assortment of 'rebels without a cause.' But that is precisely what *makes* a Rascal a Rascal: his or her *cause*. It is a cause or a dream for which a Rascal is willing to fight. The Rascal's World View is not just an intellectual exercise in economics, geopolitics, sociology, or philosophy. It is real life. It *matters*.

A Rascal, above all else (in a secular sense), cherishes his freedom and fights to preserve it, not only for himself, but for others. That is the key essence that explains the entire body of a Rascal's non-conforming behavior. It is what has been the makeup of heroes of all times and places: their sense of justice and willingness to sacrifice for their principles and for other people. To whom much is given, much is required. To whom much understanding is given, much more will be required. Once a Rascal knows the truth, there is no turning back. It is like Morpheus offering Neo the choice between the blue pill and the red pill in the movie *The Matrix*. The blue pill represented blissful ignorance, but also blind servitude. The red pill offered truth, but the battle for justice that went along with it. Neo chose the red pill and became a hero. Neo was a Rascal, because the choice he made in a fictitious movie is the same one a Rascal makes in real life every day. Rascals choose the truth and the responsibility to fight for justice that comes with it.

Ed Freeman and Bruce Crandall

The United States government was still calling the involvement of U.S. military personnel in Viet Nam a "police action," but from the intensity of the fighting in the Ia Drang Valley that day of November 14, 1965, it certainly looked like a war. Especially to the battalion of American soldiers pinned down by so much enemy fire that the medical evacuation helicopters refused to fly to their aid. Without supplies and the evacuation of the many wounded, the Americans stood the chance of being completely wiped out.

At that point, helicopter pilot Ed Freeman and his commander Bruce Crandall together decided to volunteer to fly their unarmed Hueys into Landing Zone X-Ray, a mere hundred meters or so from the perimeter of the fighting. Time after time the two men flew directly through enemy gunfire to the imperiled American soldiers. They brought water, ammunition, and medical supplies, and returned with the severely wounded. From the time the medical evacuation was halted, Freeman and Crandall made fourteen more trips into the beleaguered zone. Many on hand that day were quick to say that the entire unit might have been eliminated if not for the heroics of those two men, and the thirty wounded soldiers rescued that day most certainly would have perished.

Freeman and Crandall were considered crazy for flying again and again directly into the face of overwhelming enemy fire. But, like true Rascals, they did it anyway for the sake of their brothers in arms. Men were counting on them and they refused to let them down, no matter the risk to them personally. In the service of others they risked it all. For their uncommon valor, extraordinary heroism, and dedication to duty, Freeman and Crandall were awarded the U.S. military's highest recognition, the Medal of Honor.

CHAPTER 6

The Test

As we have seen, Rascals are different; not only from the crowd, but even from each other. They are individually individualistic. Some are more "Rascally" than others. Taking the Test of Rascalinity will let you know what level Rascal you are, where your strengths lie, and in what areas you can be working toward improvement. Also, as you grow into more of a Rascal over time, the Test of Rascalinity will help you measure progress and keep yourself on track.

Testing for Rascalinity

Observing one's behavior is the surest test of a Rascal's authenticity. Seeing a person in pressure situations, in moments where courage is required, where complacency is rampant, where freedom is under attack, is where a Rascal shows his mettle. The following test is designed to simulate actual observations of behavior. Since you, the reader, are present during every one of your own behaviors, you are the most convenient person to answer the questions presented here. Still, we are biased toward ourselves and can easily be too complimentary or too hard on ourselves. Therefore, others that you trust can also take this test with you in mind, giving interesting insight and feedback from the perspective of on outsider. This is usually helpful in identifying blind spots: those things about ourselves that are clear to others but we don't see. Also, this test is subjective and therefore not infallible, but it will provide a general range of your Rascalinity. After the test, we will review the ways in which a Rascal can increase his score.

For each of the following Rascalinity Test statements, simply answer with a 1,2,3,4, or 5, according to the following scale:

1 = not me at all
2 = rarely me
3 = true about half the time
4 = usually me
5 = *totally* me

There is a Rascalinity Test worksheet immediately following the questions. There are also more provided at the back of the book.

Rascalinity Test

2 1. I put off the good I could have today for the great I can achieve tomorrow.

4 2. I have always felt, deep down, that I was made for something great.

4 3. I always do what is right, even if it costs me.

3 4. People are often telling me to take it easy because I work so hard.

5 5. I get very angry when I see an innocent person being taken advantage of.

3 6. I can point to several key moments of peak inspiration in my life.

3 7. I have fallen in love with learning and I can't get enough.

3.2 8. I know the edges of my comfort zone and I push through them often.

3.2 9. I don't pout or hold grudges. I get the issue out on the

160

table so it can be fixed.

5   10. I can hang in there through tough times without complaint.

2   11. I have been told that I am different.

3   12. I am a sunny person.

5 4   13. I am not quick to believe what I hear on TV and in the news.

4 1   14. I have a clear vision of what I want my future to be like.

5   15. I get excited when I think about the possibility of making a difference with what I do.

5   16. My conscience really convicts me if I do something I know to be wrong.

2 1   17. I am a very driven person.

5   18. I have a very strong sense of "fair" and "unfair."

2   19. My friends would say that I am passionate.

5   20. I read good, life-enhancing books on a regular basis.

3   21. My friends would say that I am courageous.

5   22. I am a very loving person.

4   23. There are some massive struggles that have come my way and I am proud of how I made it through them.

1   24. Nowadays, I would probably be diagnosed with Attention Deficit Disorder.

4 3   25. I have a very positive attitude.

3 2   26. I am great at reading between the lines of what people say and do.

4   27. I have strong focus on the task at hand.

4   28. I live by the verse, "To whom much is given much is required."

4   29. People would say that I have character.

4 30. I believe that perfect practice makes perfect, and I live it.

2 31. I cry for the suffering of other people.

3,2 32. I have no trouble motivating myself.

2 33. People would say that I am a student of success.

3 34. I never chicken out.

2 35. I try to discover the unique characteristics of my friends, so I can serve them better.

4 36. People would say that I am very persistent.

3,2 37. I love to come up with new ideas.

4,3 38. I am not one to sink into a "pity party."

3 39. I can walk into a room and immediately ascertain the mood of the group.

4 40. I set priorities and stick to them.

3 41. I wake up in the morning thinking about my purpose and cause.

5 42. If given extra change, I always return the money.

5 43. My parents, teachers, coaches and friends would say I am a hard worker.

3 44. I am very thankful for my freedom and think about if often.

3 45. Though I sometimes have doubts, I kill them quickly.

5 46. Some of my discretionary income always goes to self-development and educational materials.

3 47. I hate to let things fester.

5 48. Most people would say that I am fun to be around.

5 49. I never quit.

3 50. I am very creative.

4 51. I am quick to find the silver lining in all things.

5 52. I am always willing to consider both sides of any

issue.

5 53. I am able to maintain a long term focus if I'm engaged in a worthwhile goal.

5 2 54. I definitely have a big dream for which I am willing to fight.

5 55. To cheat a little is the same as cheating a lot.

5 56. I have formed at least one, major productive habit in the last year.

3 57. I don't like it when people are divided up into groups for political purposes.

3 58. I do not have a problem with complacency. I am striving for more and better all the time.

5 59. I consistently feel I have a lot to learn.

3 60. When there is a problem in my life, I hit it head on.

5 61. I have learned to give a sincere apology when I am wrong.

5 62. When I make a commitment to someone, I stick with them through thick and thin.

2 63. My self-esteem is strong, because I know God made me for a purpose.

3 64. No one would say that I am a whiner or complainer.

4 65. I am usually interested in at least finding out the contrarian view on an issue.

2 66. I use visualization techniques to try and see my future more clearly.

3 2 67. I have done many selfless acts and kept them between just God and me.

5 68. I believe there is "right" and there is "wrong."

5 69. I can still remember when I learned that I could get good at something if I tried hard enough.

3 70. I am very concerned about the loss of freedom in our

society.

3 71. I know what it means to be "In the Zone", because I have often experienced it myself.

4 72. I hate being ignorant about a subject.

2 73. I have had my full share of critics in my life.

5 74. I have friends with whom I've been close for a long time.

5 75. I may get knocked down, but I always get up again.

4 76. Most of the sports or activities I have enjoyed are individual ones.

3 77. With me, the glass is always half full.

1 78. I don't usually fall for practical jokes.

3 79. I don't see things as they are, but rather as they could be.

5 80. I am more interested in who I become than the things I can accumulate.

4 81. People know if they tell me something in confidence, I will keep it secret.

4 82. The harder I work, the luckier I get.

2 83. I hate that the world is not fair.

2 84. I am not one to over-analyze.

1 85. I have a spiritual mentor.

3 86. I can name five significant times I forced myself to overcome a fear.

4 87. People know they can count on me.

2 88. My life demonstrates that almost anything worthwhile requires a long term commitment.

2 89. I march to the beat of my own drum.

3 90. My friends would say that I am a always smiling.

3 91. I am always interested in finding the deeper level of

understanding on an issue.

5 92. I have it pretty clear in mind where I want to be 10 years from now.

3 93. I am able to do what I am supposed to do even when I don't feel like it.

2 94. I would never snoop through someone else's private things.

4 95. I am good at breaking bad habits.

5 96. Each individual, each person, each life, matters.

1 97. Inaction is not one of my problems.

4 98. When I am interested in a subject, I can't learn enough about it.

3 99. One thing I know about myself is that I am not a coward.

5 100. The people that know me best would say that I am extremely loyal.

3 101. It takes a lot to discourage me.

2 102. I'm not very susceptible to the opinions of other people.

2 103. When a problem occurs, I am the one everyone looks to for a positive attitude about it.

3 104. I am good at making decisions.

3 5 105. I have goals that are written down.

5 106. I want to be a force for good in this world.

1 107. I have lost friends, because I refused to compromise my principles.

3 108. My days are disciplined.

2 109. I am committed to fight for justice.

1 110. I build the drama in my mind for the accomplishment of my goals.

3 111. I have a very curious nature.

4 112. I would rather go down in flames than cave in on what I feel is right.

5 113. I put a high priority on my friendships.

4 114. Once I have committed to something, there is no stopping me.

3 115. People who know me well would say that I am a brand all my own.

4 116. I know that no matter what happens to me, I can recover from it.

3 117. I have always had a great sense of timing.

4 118. I have no problem delaying gratification, waiting until later to buy something or do something once I've earned it.

2 3 119. Most people would call me a servant leader.

5 120. I hold being honorable as one of my most important attributes.

4 121. Hard work is a lot of fun.

5 122. I do not blame others for my problems.

4 123. I am inspired to know that my efforts impact the larger picture, and it drives me.

5 124. I always feel that there is never enough time to read.

2 125. Confronting brutal reality is not a problem for me.

3 126. I am always buying gifts, sending cards, sending texts, or reaching out to my buddies in some way.

2 127. It takes a lot to hurt my feelings.

3 128. I like to do things my own special way.

3 129. I am not a worrier.

4 130. I know that things are rarely what they seem.

Rascalinity Test Worksheet:

	A	B	C	D	E	F	G	H	I	J	K	L	M
	1. 2	2. 4	3. 4	4. 3	5. 6	6. 3	7. 3	8. 2	9. 2 3	10. 5	11. 2	12. 3	13. 4 5
	14. 4 4	15. 6	16. 5	17. 4 2	18. 5	19. 2	20. 5	21. 2	22. 4	23. 4	24. 1	25. 2 4	26. 2 3
	27. 4	28. 4	29. 3	30. 5	31. 2	32. 2 3	33. 2	34. 3	35. 2	36. 6	37. 3	38. 4	39. 2
	40. 5	41. 2 5	42. 5	43. 5	44. 5	45. 3	46. 5	47. 3	48. 5	49. 6	50. 2	51. 4	52. 5
	53. 5	54. 5	55. 5	56. 5	57. 3	58. 3	59. 5	60. 3	61. 5	62. 5	63. 2	64. 2	65. 2
	66. 2	67. 3	68. 3	69. 4	70. 2	71. 3	72. 4	73. 2	74. 5	75. 5	76. 4	77. 3	78. 1
	79. 4	80. 5	81. 4	82. 4	83. 2	84. 2	85. 1	86. 3	87. 4	88. 2	89. 2	90. 3	91. 3
	92. 3 3	93. 3	94. 2	95. 4	96. 4	97. 1	98. 4	99. 3	100. 4	101. 3	102. 3	103. 2	104. 3
	105. 3	106. 5	107. 1	108. 3	109. 3	110. 5	111. 3	112. 4	113. 5	114. 4	115. 3	116. 4	117. 2
	118. 4	119. 3 2	120. 5	121. 4	122. 5	123. 4	124. 5	125. 2	126. 3	127. 2	128. 3	129. 3	130. 4
Totals:	31 34n	26 39n	40n	28 39n	35n	24 26	37n	28n	41 11n	39n	24 25n	21 33n	31 34n
Category:	A	B	C	D	E	F	G	H	I	J	K	L	M

Grand Total: 443 c
462 n

Level of Rascalinity

This part of the test is rather easy and straight forward. In fact, being a Rascal, you have probably already added up the score of each column and then arrived at a grand total. And you have also probably looked below to the scale indicating your overall level of Rascalinity! Since we know you are going to rush ahead and do it anyway, let's look at those levels now.

Grand Total	Level of Rascalinity
0 to 192	**Rascal Wanna-Be**, but don't give up hope
193 to 355	**Rookie Rascal**, keep learning and growing
356 to 486	**Mid-Pack Rascal**, glad to have you with us
487 to 584	**Leading Rascal**, you're incredible
585 to 650	**Legendary Rascal**, the elite of the elite

Understanding Your Score

Now that you know your Level of Rascalinity you can use it as a yard stick with which to measure your future progress as you grow into even more of a Rascal. After all, don't we all want to become more Rascally, become better, and make a bigger contribution?

Assuming that the answer for you is "yes," there is more that can be learned from your score to help you on your journey. Having a grand total and a corresponding label for your present level is good. Understanding how to capitalize on it will take you to the next level.

First, let's consider two ways of looking at strengths and weaknesses. There are those who will tell you to ignore your weaknesses and focus on your strengths, allowing your weaknesses to die from starvation. Others will tell you success is all about fixing your problems so they no longer hold you back. As with most things in life, the truth is a mix of the two viewpoints.

Certainly we don't want to over-fixate on our problems. Doing so causes us to pull our focus away from the areas where we are naturally endowed, depletes our confidence, and drains our motivation. However, if the weaknesses are large enough, they can smother any chance the strengths have of moving us forward. In particular, if our weaknesses are weaknesses of character, they *must* be addressed immediately or the kind of success and significance for which a Rascal longs will never be realized. For some people, their weaknesses are so prevalent that they must be fixed in order to succeed any further. This is why it is helpful to have someone else take the test on your behalf. It might just point out some blind spots for which you are not aware. However, do this carefully, and only with people for whom you have the highest trust and respect. We should always invite "constructive" criticism carefully, as it *is* still *criticism*, and no matter how much of a Rascal we are, we can only handle so much of it.

> **If the weaknesses are large enough, they can smother any chance the strengths have of moving us forward.**

If you do have others take the test with you in mind, then you might want to average their score for you with the one you came up with for yourself. Or, if there are any areas where they strongly differ from your own assessments, apply those to what we will discuss next and use that to identify key areas on which to work, but also, areas where it appears you are the strongest.

The columns on the worksheet you completed represent categories of Rascalinity. This is not an exact science, of course, as many of the questions could apply to more than one category. However, they are purposefully arranged to emphasize the main thrust for each statement in the test. With that said, let's first determine where your strengths lie.

Here's the key to the columns and their represented categories:

A: Vision/Focus/Delayed Gratification
B: Purpose/Meaning/Dream
C: Character/Honor
D: Work Ethic/Mastery/Habits
E: Justice
F: Inspiration
G: Hunger to Learn
H: Courage
I: Relationships
J: Perseverance/Commitment/Toughness
K: Individuality
L: Attitude
M: Discernment

The totaled score of each column represents the comparative strength. The higher the score, the stronger you are in that category. In the spaces below, write the three categories in which you received the highest total score.

Biggest Strength Category *RELATIONSHIPS*

Second Biggest Strength Category *CHARACTER, HONOR*

Third Biggest Strength Category *TIE-* *PERSEVERANCE / COMMITMENT / TOUGHNESS*
AND PURPOSE

There is something very empowering about receiving clear feedback on our strengths and then writing them down. Allow this to encourage you and embolden you on your path to greater Rascalinity.

Next we will consider weaknesses. We will use the same method and worksheet as we did to determine strengths. This time, however, look at the columns or categories with the lowest totals. Record the two lowest categories below.

Biggest Area for Improvement _TIE: JUSTICE & INDIVIDUALITY_
INSPIRATION &   _"_

Second Biggest Area for Improvement _COURAGE_

Notice we are not calling these weaknesses now but rather "areas for improvement." This is because they aren't weaknesses if you address them. Rascals are committed to growing personally and maximizing their potential, therefore weaknesses, if addressed head-on, do not remain so. They become areas of personal growth.

Do not become demoralized when looking at these categories. Remember, none of us is perfect and if we take this test and end up with no areas for improvement, we are either very far along on the journey to Rascalinity, or we have an overblown image of ourselves and weren't being accurate when taking the test.

The first thing to do with this information is to determine the magnitude of the two areas for improvement you've identified. The most serious are those involving Character and Honor. If this is one of your categories for improvement, as I said before, it must be addressed immediately. Perhaps the second most critical area for improvement to address is Courage. It is almost impossible to fully develop Character and Honor if courage is lacking. Again, hit this one head on and with no delay. The remaining categories are also important, but are not as foundational as Character/Honor and

Courage. Determine the magnitude of weakness in each of your areas for improvement. For instance, were there a lot of 1's or 2's for each of these two categories or just a couple? Did other people agree when they took this test on your behalf? Remember, we don't want to focus too much on our weaknesses, but they do need to be shored up as much as possible without distracting us from our strengths.

When it comes to growing our strengths, this is normally easy and fun. After all, it aligns with our most natural abilities and affinities anyway. The key concept to understand is that you will succeed the biggest, make the largest impact, and create the most significant legacy if you find a way to live within the categories of your biggest strengths. This is easy to forget, as the world, other people, and responsibilities love to pull us in conflicting directions. Rascals, however, know to stay firmly rooted in their areas of strength. They take what they've been given and maximize it to their full potential.

So How Does a Rascal Grow in Rascalinity?

Rascals realize they can grow in their Rascalinity, becoming more effective and significant, experiencing greater degrees of freedom and empowerment in their lives. There are many action steps that can grow a Rascal's character and make his life more fulfilling and intentional. Below are several:

1. Think about your life's purpose, and write down your thoughts.

2. Ponder and obtain answers for life's eternal questions, understanding your spiritual life and your standing before your Creator.

3. Identify causes that make you come alive and for which you would sacrifice.

4. Determine how you can serve the people in your life.

5. Clearly define the biggest dreams you have for your life, and write them down.

6. Set clear goals in the pursuit of your dreams, and put deadlines on their accomplishment.

7. Become a life-long learner, making the reading of good books and the Scriptures a habit (see the categorized Recommended Reading List at the back of this book).

8. Find a mentor to keep you accountable and on track.

9. Take steps daily to build relationships and expand your network of allies and contacts, associating regularly with other Rascals.

10. Schedule time for restoration and renewal.

11. Write down your life's priorities and review them often.

12. Periodically take the Test of Rascalinity to track your progress.

13. Take action NOW!

Growing as a person is what being a Rascal is all about. Without a heart change, without getting our eternal questions in order and understanding the bigger picture of our world and how we fit into it, we will never maximize and fulfill our true potential. In fact, we will never truly live. A Rascal intentionally emphasizes his strengths and assassinates his weaknesses so that he can maximize his contribution. It is not easy, but Rascals are not interested in ease. They do what needs to be done in order to maximize their impact as a force for good and live a life that counts. Growing means that even though they may not have everything it takes today, Rascals can come back tomorrow a little stronger and a little better.

Gerrold Mor

For hundreds of years, England held sway over Ireland. Their hegemony ranged from tyranny and brutal murder to loose control, but always, generation after generation, there was the yoke of English rule. Lands were taken from peasants and given to rich English nobles. Religious war and cruelty were common. Favoritism, power hunger, greed, fraud, and nepotism dominated the governance of the island. But always and throughout, there was strong resistance to English rule and defiant rebellion led by courageous Rascals.

Thomas FitzGerald, the eighth earl of Kildare, whom the Irish called Gerrold Mor, was an Englishman through and through. He'd married a cousin of the King of England, and with his induction into the Order of the Garter, he'd been awarded one of the king's highest honors. But consistent with a long line of English nobleman in Ireland, he would also be accused of being more Irish than English, becoming instrumental in Ireland's resistance to English domination.

Mor served as the English governor of Ireland for more than thirty years, but he did so by twice openly defying English kings. In 1478, when emissaries from King Edward IV were sent to Ireland to replace him, Mor simply refused. Then in 1488 Mor did it again. By 1494 the English monarchy had had enough, and king Henry VII sent an army to Ireland to capture power from Mor and arrest him. After a period, Mor was released, but only under the condition that he leave his son behind in England as a pledge of loyalty and insurance of obedience.

Mor's willful stands against England made him very popular in Ireland. But he was also fiercely opposed by other factions on the island. A tireless politician, Mor built strong alliances with Gaelic chieftains, and used military might to defeat his enemies. As one English king said of him, "He is meet to rule all Ireland, seeing as all Ireland cannot rule him." In fact, it was his near total sway over the island that fostered the jealousy of the English kings.

As a ruler, Mor did much for the cause of unifying the many factions of Ireland. He also helped usher in the Renaissance in Ireland by aiding in the establishment of libraries and schools, and he encouraged Gaelic art and literature.

As a Rascal on an island of Rascals, Mor was impressive with his accomplishments of unification and resistance to English dominance. As Malachy McCourt wrote, "Gerrold Mor had ruled Kildare and the English pale for nearly forty years, and for the most part had remained a popular ruler during the entirety. He had kept a large range of English kings from meddling too drastically in the affairs of Ireland and had stretched his influence over much of the island. Gerrold Mor was surely his own man, and he began a family dynasty that would result in proud Anglo-Irish defiance."

CHAPTER 7

The Manifesto

In the battle for excellence, Obstacès and his Jackals will stand as staunch adversaries. Trying to do great things is always met with resistance. It's a bit like lifting weights. The weight that is lifted is actually what builds the muscles. Success is similar. It is the problems and challenges overcome by the Rascal that determine the magnitude and credibility of the success achieved.

This means that for any would-be Rascal there are tough times ahead. There will be moments of doubt, setbacks and frustrations. Many people will not understand your journey or your vision. You will receive offers to "wimpify" along the way. You will be tempted to cave in to your discouragement. And you will be haunted by a nagging sense of self-doubt. This is the normal landscape for a champion. In fact, *everybody*, those pursuing excellence as well as those bathing in mediocrity, will have problems. The Bible says that it rains on the just and unjust alike, but it also rains on those trying to accomplish great things *and* those doing nothing. So one might as well charge at life full of vigor and determination, committed to excellence and contribution.

Positive Affirmation

Knowing a little about the coming landscape then, what do you do when things get tough? How do you handle it when you've taken shot after shot and just don't feel like you can get back up and try again? Where do you go when all the standard things you've done to propel yourself forward just don't seem to be working any-more? There are a lot of ways to answer the challenge, includ-ing maintaining a proper perspective, keeping one's eyes upon the dream, getting around encouraging books and people, and prayer.

Also, one can program the mind to be tougher. One can hard-wire in a chord of success to be played over and over again to strengthen re-solve and push oneself forward. It's called positive affirmation. What we say to ourselves on a regular ba-sis has lasting implications. If our self-talk is critical, destructive, and doubt-filled, so too will be our actions and results. Shad Helmstet-ter wrote, "As much as seventy-five percent or more of everything that is recorded and stored in our subconscious minds is counter-productive and works against us - in short, we are programmed *not* to succeed!" If this is true, it stands to reason that we should undo the *destructive* programming in our minds and replace it with *con-structive* programming. We do this by learning to choose carefully the words we say and think to ourselves.

> **What we say to ourselves on a regular basis has lasting implications.**

The first time I encountered this technique I thought it was a little silly. It seemed strange that we should go around talking to ourselves. But then I began taking note of the thoughts I allowed to run through my brain each and every day, and I was shocked! There was a lot of negative, self-deprecating junk flitting around in there. So I determined to give it a try. I began by trying to stop negative thoughts from flowing, but that alone wasn't effec-tive. I learned that I had to replace the negative thoughts with positive ones. A substitution was required, good for bad. When this seemed to work, I learned there were statements and scriptures I could memorize and have at instant recall to use in a split second to replace negative with positive. After a while, I didn't need to wait for a negative thought before thinking a positive one; I began injecting positive statements regularly anyway. And much to my amazement, it worked! Again according to Helmstetter, "If you want to manage yourself in a better way, and change your results, you can do so at any time you choose. Start with the first step. Change your programming."

Personal, Positive Affirmation Statement

I would highly recommend you memorize scripture verses that speak to your heart. Also, pull phrases and statements from good books. Beyond that, though, it is also a good idea to craft a personal statement that speaks directly to you, reminding yourself of your future greatness and the potential you have inside. This is called a personal, positive affirmation statement.

A positive affirmation statement can be short or long, and there is nothing wrong with having several. The key is to program your thoughts in a positive direction. You will go in the direction of your most dominant thoughts, so they might as well be victorious and bold. Word your affirmation statements as though you have already brought to fruition the highest picture you have for yourself in each category. In other words, it's not "I am working to become better," or "I will become great," but rather, "I *am* the best in this field," or "I *am* making an enormous contribution," or "I *am* an awesome father and husband." Also, for them to be empowering, personal affirmation statements must be clear and specific. Consider the areas of your life such as spiritual, family, friends, fitness, finances, professional, and the like, and include in your statement how you measure up in these areas. Most importantly, however, be sure to include your most dominant and passionate dreams. Remember, you have to

> **You will go in the direction of your most dominant thoughts, so they might as well be victorious and bold.**

convince yourself you are worthy of achieving that vision you carry in your mind's eye. Having the audacity to believe that you belong there, that you can achieve it, that you can take your place among the greats in that endeavor, is the requisite step to making it a reality. You've got to see it in your mind before you get there in reality. And, you've got to believe it in your heart before you strive for it completely and with commitment. So write it down and repeat it to yourself all the time to build that future picture and belief.

Some people find this exercise difficult. My wife, for instance, had trouble with this concept until she phrased her affirmations in terms of what the Lord had done for her. Not wishing to be bold and prideful, she decided to give God the glory for her dreams and strengths, wording her affirmations accordingly. One such example is, "God made me great. If I thought any less, I'd be insulting my Creator. It is through Him that I can do all things." That's some significant positive affirmation!

The Rascal Manifesto

If you've identified with the Rascal character in this book at all, then it may also behoove you to use the following Rascal Manifesto in your positive affirmations. The purpose of the Rascal Manifesto is to remind yourself you are different, you were made for something great, and you stand out from the crowd because of what you stand for.

I was born free and I intend to live like it.
This means that I will live my life while I'm alive.

No one owns me except my Creator.
No one can put me in a box, a category, a social group,
a voting bloc, or a classification.
I am fiercely independent, and with those aligned with

me in common purpose, interdependent.
I know that with my freedom comes responsibility.
I take responsibility for my own actions, and I hold the
bar high on myself.
I am not afraid to struggle, because it's the struggle that
makes me great.
I know that excellence always lies on the other side of
inconvenience.

I am a learning machine.
I read, I confront brutal reality, I grow.
Long term, no one and nothing can defeat me, because
I will keep coming back, stronger and better than
before.

I will educate myself about the true principles of freedom, and I will strive mightily to preserve freedom for
the next generation.
I rely on no man and no government to provide for me.
I will not follow the herd of mediocrity and
victim-thinking.
I don't follow herds, instead I run with a pack - a pack
of Rascals.

Let others bask in their privileges, as for me, I will
invest them in my purpose.
I will defy tyranny.
I will charge the hill.
I will make a difference.
I'm a Rascal!

I would recommend printing this manifesto and posting it in
prominent places. There is a copy included in the back of the book

intended for this purpose. Simply tear it out. Or visit www.rascal-book.com and obtain a free download.

Wica Mnaiciyapi, Gathering the Warriors

As we began this book with Crazy Horse it only seems fitting to end it with him. In the summer of 1876 a massive gathering of Lakota and other peoples had assembled at Ash Creek at the behest of the much respected leader Sitting Bull and in response to the United States government's January 1st ultimatum which declared that any tribe not reporting in to a reservation would be considered hostile. Many groups began arriving at Sitting Bull's "unity camp" as a result of hunger or defeat at the hands of soldiers. Others were lured from the reservations. What resulted was an enormous assemblage of disparate people committed to their way of life. It was the largest gathering any of them had seen in their lifetimes.

Sitting Bull was an extremely competent leader, capable of unifying so many factions into one group. He spoke often to the leaders and elderly and worked tirelessly for unification and a show of strength through numbers against the white man. Then word came in from the scouts that a column of soldiers was approaching from the south some fifty miles away. What should be done?

Sitting Bull had amassed a great coalition of people living away from the reservations and remaining free in defiance of the ultimatum. Now things were coming to a head. Would the various tribes unite and fight together, or scatter back to the reservations or their home lands? Sitting Bull was an elderly leader and no longer a military one. Military leadership would have to come from someone else. Crazy Horse, however, had a much respected reputation as a powerful and successful warrior. When word of the approaching enemy came in, Crazy Horse did something both symbolic and militarily significant. He gathered his weapons, put on his war paint, took the food and water prepared for him by his wife, gathered both his war horses, and began to ride out from the camp. As he rode around its enormous perimeter other warriors came out to join him. The dust thickened as the number of warriors grew. Perhaps author John M. Marshall III describes the scene the best:

> "As he finished the second turn around the encampment and began the third, the old ones watching realized what Crazy Horse was doing. He was invoking an old ritual known as 'Gathering the Warriors.' Word spread quickly as more and more men joined the growing procession. It seemed as though everyone in camp stopped whatever they were doing to watch. Women began to sing the Strong Heart songs to encourage their fighting men. As the fourth and final turn around the encampment began, it was difficult to see where the procession of fighting men started and where it ended. It encircled the entire camp."

The united warriors rode all through the night and fought for over ten hours the next day, bringing the combined forces of their enemies, including US soldiers, Crow, and Snake Indians to a halt, at what is now known as the Battle of the Rosebud. Eight days later these same men would defeat Custer at the Battle of the Little Big Horn.

The *Wica Mnaiciyapi* ritual performed by Crazy Horse was a dramatic moment. It galvanized the different tribes and groups into one fighting force and compelled them to two incredible victories. Each warrior was an individual, but he had voluntarily committed his life to a fight for principles each of them shared. Their common purpose of freedom and justice had united them.

Their common purpose of freedom and justice had united them.

At this seminal moment in Crazy Horse's life he gave us an inspiring picture of how a Rascal lives. He left behind the comfort and ease of the camp and rode out to battle for the principles he held dear. He rallied others to his cause and compelled them to action. He flew boldly into the face of conflict because it was just and right, giving himself to the protection of those who could not defend themselves. He stood on principle, and fought for justice. We have learned in these pages that Rascals don't run with the herd, but as Crazy Horse demonstrated, they do protect it. To whom much is given, much is expected.

Crazy Horse is the consummate Rascal. He embodies nearly all the principles of the heroic figure, possessing the character to be a character, not for the sake of non-conformity, but for the sake of a higher calling. Crazy Horse had the strength of conviction to live his life according to his own inner voice. And if Crazy Horse is the perfect example of a Rascal, then my prayer is that this book is the embodiment of the *Wica Mnaiciyapi* ritual of "Gathering the Warriors" that he performed. May it call you out from the camp of complacency and mediocrity to join the other Rascals circling and gathering. We are stirring up dust, storming into battle, bent on defending those who can't defend themselves, and in preserving the freedoms and ways of life into which we were born. We are circling the camp and calling you to action. Will you join us? Will you mount up and ride out into a great calling, fighting for the truths in which you believe and against the injustices in your world? Will you summon the courage of conviction that resides deep within you and *develop the character to be a character?* We hope you do, because freedom is under attack by Obstacès and his Jackals, and they must be defeated.

> **Freedom has always been won, defended, and passed along by Rascals.**

That's why I wrote this book. I want to recruit you to live the exciting, courageous, purpose-filled life of a Rascal. I want to invite you to join the growing tribes of people who have the character to be characters and the convictions to be originals. Freedom depends upon it. Freedom has always been won, defended, and passed along by Rascals. But freedom's light doesn't burn as brightly as it once did; some would say it's been reduced to a mere flicker. The cause of freedom needs your help! It will require you to be crazy, in a sacred kind of way.

Recommended Reading

Character/Honor

- *Character Counts*; Os Guinness

- *Winners Never Cheat: Everyday Values We Learned as Children (But May Have Forgotten)*, Jon M. Huntsman

Purpose/Meaning/Dream

- *Wake Up Your Dreams*, Walt Kallestad

- *Season of Life: A Football Star, A Boy, A Journey to Manhood*, Jeffrey Marx

- *Put Your Dream to the Test*, John C. Maxwell

Individuality

- *The Greatest Miracle in the World*, Og Mandino

- *The Amazing Law of Influence*, King Duncan

Courage

- *Courage: The Backbone of Leadership*, Gus Lee

- *Footprints in Time: Fulfilling God's Destiny for Your Life*, Jeff O' Leary

Inspiration

- *Critical Choices That Change Lives: How Heroes Turn Tragedy Into Triumph*, Daniel R. Castro

- *The Go-Giver: A Little Story About a Powerful Business Idea*, Bob Burg and John David Mann

- *The Dash: Making a Difference with Your Life*, Linda Ellis and Mac Anderson

Vision/Focus/Delayed Gratification

- *The Laws of Lifetime Growth: Always Make Your Future Bigger Than Your Past*, Dan Sullivan and Catherine Nomura

- *The Psychology of Winning: Ten Qualities of a Total Winner*, Dr. Denis Waitley

Perseverance/Commitment/Toughness

- *Unstoppable: 45 Powerful Stories of Perseverance and Triumph from People Just Like You*, Cynthia Kersey

- *Outliers: The Story of Success*, Malcolm Gladwell

Attitude

- *Attitude is Everything: Change Your Attitude . . . And You Change Your Life!*, Jeff Keller

- *The Ultimate Gift*, Jim Stovall

Hunger to Learn

- *Live, Learn, Lead to Make a Difference*, Don Soderquist

- *The Magic of Thinking Big*, David J. Schwartz, Ph.D.

Justice

- *Profiles in Audacity: Great Decisions and How They Were Made*, Alan Axelrod

- *Leading Quietly: An Unorthodox Guide to Doing the Right Thing*, Joseph L. Badaracco, Jr.

Relationships

- *The Speed of Trust: The One Thing That Changes Everything*, Stephen M. R. Covey

- *Balcony People*, Joyce Landorf Heatherly

- *How to Win Friends and Influence People*, Dale Carnegie

Discernment

- *Wrong! the Biggest Mistakes and Miscalculations Ever made by People Who Should Have Known Better*, Jane O'Boyle

- *A Whack on the Side of the Head: How You Can Be More Creative*, Roger von Oech

Work Ethic/Mastery/Habits

- *Talent Is Overrated,* Geoff Colvin

- *The Slight Edge,* Jeff Olsen

Glossary of Terms

A Force For Good - the desire of every Rascal ('Good' as opposed to evil, not to be confused with the 'Good' that is the enemy of Great. That is a different meaning and you shouldn't be trying to confuse the author who is perfectly capable of that on his own).

Blind Spots - those things about ourselves that are clear to others but we don't see in ourselves

Blue Pill - from the movie *The Matrix*; represents blissful ignorance, but also blind servitude

B.U.R. - behavior unbecoming of a Rascal

Busyness - the condition of being swamped by the urgent but unimportant

Character Failures - the most serious challenge to any Rascal

Communism, Socialism, Collectivism, and Statism - the most dangerous "isms" in the entire species, opposed to freedom for the individual and always resulting in barbed wire fences, machine guns, search lights, and patrol boats to force people into 'enjoying the benefits.'

Complacency - the near national epidemic of people thinking they're "doing pretty good."

Cowardice - the behavior of the braggart, who beats his chest the hardest but heads for cover as soon as the ammunition is real

Delayed Gratification - the nearly extinct concept of denying one's self until something has been earned

Discouragement - the opposite of encouragement

Distraction - majoring on minors

Doubt - the condition of re-analyzing something one has already decided upon. This only occurs when fortitude is lacking.

Faustian Bargain - from Thomas Mann's classic, *Doctor Faustus*, in which a man sells his soul to the Devil in exchange for fame and fortune in this life.

Fear - an acronym; False Evidence Appearing Real

fortes fortuna adiuvat - Latin; translated as either "forts for tuna audio vat," meaning a place where fish can hide and listen to music, or the more common translation; "Fortune favors the bold."

Freedom - the rare condition whereby a person is free to live his or her own life and choose his or her own destiny, without untoward interference from anybody or any *body* (as in group or government, etc.)

Good - the enemy of Great.

Hard Work - the key to obtaining mastery.

Honor - the ancient custom of being in reality who you represent yourself to be

Hunger - the healthy attributes of ambition which drive a Rascal to become better

Interdependence - Independence raised to the level of teamwork

Jackal - a person who was once on the path to being a Rascal, but went through the Wimpification Process of excuses, justification, and blame, and transforms into a critic of Rascals.

Justify - to lament, as in "just if I" would have done what I should have!

Leadership Revolution - (also known as a Rascalution) the condition that results from people making individual decisions to take responsibility for leading right where they are, with who they are and with what they have.

Leading Rascal - any person who scores between 487 and 584 on the Test of Rascalinity

Legendary Rascal - any person who scores between 585 and 650 on the Test of Rascalinity

Mastery - the product of applied and focused perfect practice over a long period of time (shown by some studies to be 10,000 hours)

Mid-Pack Rascal - any person who scores between 356 and 486 on the Test of Rascalinity

Obstacles - the chief nemesis of any Rascal. This spiny-headed creature never sleeps, and gets his greatest rewards from causing Rascals to stumble and fall. He also has a shamelessly poor physique.

Perseverance - the quality of hanging on long after the wimps have been shaken off

Positive Attitude - the opposite condition from that possessed by your in-laws

Principles - those pesky absolute truths that defy anyone who dares not follow them

Rascal-Dazzle - a really creative word I should have used in the book but didn't

Rascal Frenchman - my relative who was responsible for inspiring this whole concept in the first place

Rascalinity - the degree to which a person exhibits Rascal-like behavior

Rascalution - the productive result that occurs each time an external, unjust stimulus presses in on a concentration of Rascals (e.g. the American Revolution)

Rascal Wanna-Be - any person who scores between 0 and 192 on the Test of Rascalinity

Rationalize - to tell rational lies

Red Pill - from the movie *The Matrix*; represents irreversible knowledge of truth, but the battle for justice that goes along with it

Romantic Battle - the difficulties of your journey seen from the proper, dramatic perspective

Rookie Rascal - any person who scores between 193 and 355 on the Test of Rascalinity

The Productive Loop - the process whereby a Rascal accomplishes great things and astounds his critics

They - the thought police, the guardians of political correctness, the masters of conformity, the keepers of the status quo

The Zone - a concept that describes a peak performer in a moment all their own, where they are doing exactly what God built them to do, to the best of their ability, with all of their faculties aligned and intensely focused. (It can also mean the spot where tickling is the most effective).

Thumb Sucking - the substitute activity people do when they Wimpify (okay, I couldn't fit this in the book anywhere, but it is still important to know)

Wimpification - the process of chickening out from a worthy endeavor. Also known as rolling over on one's self, playing the ninny, being a coward, and quitting.

World View - represents the lens through which we see the world around us. It involves how we perceive truth, what we think of life's ultimate questions, the principles in which we believe, our faith life, and any other major contributors to how life is perceived and interpreted by our minds.

You - someone who has more potential than is even realized

Rascalinity Test Worksheet:

A	B	C	D	E	F	G	H	I	J	K	L	M
1. ___	2. ___	3. ___	4. ___	5. ___	6. ___	7. ___	8. ___	9. ___	10. ___	11. ___	12. ___	13. ___
14. ___	15. ___	16. ___	17. ___	18. ___	19. ___	20. ___	21. ___	22. ___	23. ___	24. ___	25. ___	26. ___
27. ___	28. ___	29. ___	30. ___	31. ___	32. ___	33. ___	34. ___	35. ___	36. ___	37. ___	38. ___	39. ___
40. ___	41. ___	42. ___	43. ___	44. ___	45. ___	46. ___	47. ___	48. ___	49. ___	50. ___	51. ___	52. ___
53. ___	54. ___	55. ___	56. ___	57. ___	58. ___	59. ___	60. ___	61. ___	62. ___	63. ___	64. ___	65. ___
66. ___	67. ___	68. ___	69. ___	70. ___	71. ___	72. ___	73. ___	74. ___	75. ___	76. ___	77. ___	78. ___
79. ___	80. ___	81. ___	82. ___	83. ___	84. ___	85. ___	86. ___	87. ___	88. ___	89. ___	90. ___	91. ___
92. ___	93. ___	94. ___	95. ___	96. ___	97. ___	98. ___	99. ___	100. ___	101. ___	102. ___	103. ___	104. ___
105. ___	106. ___	107. ___	108. ___	109. ___	110. ___	111. ___	112. ___	113. ___	114. ___	115. ___	116. ___	117. ___
118. ___	119. ___	120. ___	121. ___	122. ___	123. ___	124. ___	125. ___	126. ___	127. ___	128. ___	129. ___	130. ___

Totals:
Category: A___ B___ C___ D___ E___ F___ G___ H___ I___ J___ K___ L___ M___

Grand Total: ___

Rascalinity Test Worksheet:

1. ___	2. ___	3. ___	4. ___	5. ___	6. ___	7. ___	8. ___	9. ___	10. ___	11. ___	12. ___	13. ___
14. ___	15. ___	16. ___	17. ___	18. ___	19. ___	20. ___	21. ___	22. ___	23. ___	24. ___	25. ___	26. ___
27. ___	28. ___	29. ___	30. ___	31. ___	32. ___	33. ___	34. ___	35. ___	36. ___	37. ___	38. ___	39. ___
40. ___	41. ___	42. ___	43. ___	44. ___	45. ___	46. ___	47. ___	48. ___	49. ___	50. ___	51. ___	52. ___
53. ___	54. ___	55. ___	56. ___	57. ___	58. ___	59. ___	60. ___	61. ___	62. ___	63. ___	64. ___	65. ___
66. ___	67. ___	68. ___	69. ___	70. ___	71. ___	72. ___	73. ___	74. ___	75. ___	76. ___	77. ___	78. ___
79. ___	80. ___	81. ___	82. ___	83. ___	84. ___	85. ___	86. ___	87. ___	88. ___	89. ___	90. ___	91. ___
92. ___	93. ___	94. ___	95. ___	96. ___	97. ___	98. ___	99. ___	100. ___	101. ___	102. ___	103. ___	104. ___
105. ___	106. ___	107. ___	108. ___	109. ___	110. ___	111. ___	112. ___	113. ___	114. ___	115. ___	116. ___	117. ___
118. ___	119. ___	120. ___	121. ___	122. ___	123. ___	124. ___	125. ___	126. ___	127. ___	128. ___	129. ___	130. ___

Totals:

Category:	A	B	C	D	E	F	G	H	I	J	K	L	M

Grand Total: _____

Rascalinity Test Worksheet:

A	B	C	D	E	F	G	H	I	J	K	L	M
1. ___	2. ___	3. ___	4. ___	5. ___	6. ___	7. ___	8. ___	9. ___	10. ___	11. ___	12. ___	13. ___
14. ___	15. ___	16. ___	17. ___	18. ___	19. ___	20. ___	21. ___	22. ___	23. ___	24. ___	25. ___	26. ___
27. ___	28. ___	29. ___	30. ___	31. ___	32. ___	33. ___	34. ___	35. ___	36. ___	37. ___	38. ___	39. ___
40. ___	41. ___	42. ___	43. ___	44. ___	45. ___	46. ___	47. ___	48. ___	49. ___	50. ___	51. ___	52. ___
53. ___	54. ___	55. ___	56. ___	57. ___	58. ___	59. ___	60. ___	61. ___	62. ___	63. ___	64. ___	65. ___
66. ___	67. ___	68. ___	69. ___	70. ___	71. ___	72. ___	73. ___	74. ___	75. ___	76. ___	77. ___	78. ___
79. ___	80. ___	81. ___	82. ___	83. ___	84. ___	85. ___	86. ___	87. ___	88. ___	89. ___	90. ___	91. ___
92. ___	93. ___	94. ___	95. ___	96. ___	97. ___	98. ___	99. ___	100. ___	101. ___	102. ___	103. ___	104. ___
105. ___	106. ___	107. ___	108. ___	109. ___	110. ___	111. ___	112. ___	113. ___	114. ___	115. ___	116. ___	117. ___
118. ___	119. ___	120. ___	121. ___	122. ___	123. ___	124. ___	125. ___	126. ___	127. ___	128. ___	129. ___	130. ___

Totals:
Category: A ___ B ___ C ___ D ___ E ___ F ___ G ___ H ___ I ___ J ___ K ___ L ___ M ___

Grand Total: ___

Rascalinity Test Worksheet:

	A	B	C	D	E	F	G	H	I	J	K	L	M
	1. ___	2. ___	3. ___	4. ___	5. ___	6. ___	7. ___	8. ___	9. ___	10. ___	11. ___	12. ___	13. ___
	14. ___	15. ___	16. ___	17. ___	18. ___	19. ___	20. ___	21. ___	22. ___	23. ___	24. ___	25. ___	26. ___
	27. ___	28. ___	29. ___	30. ___	31. ___	32. ___	33. ___	34. ___	35. ___	36. ___	37. ___	38. ___	39. ___
	40. ___	41. ___	42. ___	43. ___	44. ___	45. ___	46. ___	47. ___	48. ___	49. ___	50. ___	51. ___	52. ___
	53. ___	54. ___	55. ___	56. ___	57. ___	58. ___	59. ___	60. ___	61. ___	62. ___	63. ___	64. ___	65. ___
	66. ___	67. ___	68. ___	69. ___	70. ___	71. ___	72. ___	73. ___	74. ___	75. ___	76. ___	77. ___	78. ___
	79. ___	80. ___	81. ___	82. ___	83. ___	84. ___	85. ___	86. ___	87. ___	88. ___	89. ___	90. ___	91. ___
	92. ___	93. ___	94. ___	95. ___	96. ___	97. ___	98. ___	99. ___	100. ___	101. ___	102. ___	103. ___	104. ___
	105. ___	106. ___	107. ___	108. ___	109. ___	110. ___	111. ___	112. ___	113. ___	114. ___	115. ___	116. ___	117. ___
	118. ___	119. ___	120. ___	121. ___	122. ___	123. ___	124. ___	125. ___	126. ___	127. ___	128. ___	129. ___	130. ___

Totals:
Category: A   B   C   D   E   F   G   H   I   J   K   L   M

Grand Total: ___

Rascalinity Test Worksheet:

	A	B	C	D	E	F	G	H	I	J	K	L	M
	1. ___	2. ___	3. ___	4. ___	5. ___	6. ___	7. ___	8. ___	9. ___	10. ___	11. ___	12. ___	13. ___
	14. ___	15. ___	16. ___	17. ___	18. ___	19. ___	20. ___	21. ___	22. ___	23. ___	24. ___	25. ___	26. ___
	27. ___	28. ___	29. ___	30. ___	31. ___	32. ___	33. ___	34. ___	35. ___	36. ___	37. ___	38. ___	39. ___
	40. ___	41. ___	42. ___	43. ___	44. ___	45. ___	46. ___	47. ___	48. ___	49. ___	50. ___	51. ___	52. ___
	53. ___	54. ___	55. ___	56. ___	57. ___	58. ___	59. ___	60. ___	61. ___	62. ___	63. ___	64. ___	65. ___
	66. ___	67. ___	68. ___	69. ___	70. ___	71. ___	72. ___	73. ___	74. ___	75. ___	76. ___	77. ___	78. ___
	79. ___	80. ___	81. ___	82. ___	83. ___	84. ___	85. ___	86. ___	87. ___	88. ___	89. ___	90. ___	91. ___
	92. ___	93. ___	94. ___	95. ___	96. ___	97. ___	98. ___	99. ___	100. ___	101. ___	102. ___	103. ___	104. ___
	105. ___	106. ___	107. ___	108. ___	109. ___	110. ___	111. ___	112. ___	113. ___	114. ___	115. ___	116. ___	117. ___
	118. ___	119. ___	120. ___	121. ___	122. ___	123. ___	124. ___	125. ___	126. ___	127. ___	128. ___	129. ___	130. ___
Totals:													
Category:	A	B	C	D	E	F	G	H	I	J	K	L	M

Grand Total: ___

Rascalinity Test Worksheet:

A	B	C	D	E	F	G	H	I	J	K	L	M
1. ___	2. ___	3. ___	4. ___	5. ___	6. ___	7. ___	8. ___	9. ___	10. ___	11. ___	12. ___	13. ___
14. ___	15. ___	16. ___	17. ___	18. ___	19. ___	20. ___	21. ___	22. ___	23. ___	24. ___	25. ___	26. ___
27. ___	28. ___	29. ___	30. ___	31. ___	32. ___	33. ___	34. ___	35. ___	36. ___	37. ___	38. ___	39. ___
40. ___	41. ___	42. ___	43. ___	44. ___	45. ___	46. ___	47. ___	48. ___	49. ___	50. ___	51. ___	52. ___
53. ___	54. ___	55. ___	56. ___	57. ___	58. ___	59. ___	60. ___	61. ___	62. ___	63. ___	64. ___	65. ___
66. ___	67. ___	68. ___	69. ___	70. ___	71. ___	72. ___	73. ___	74. ___	75. ___	76. ___	77. ___	78. ___
79. ___	80. ___	81. ___	82. ___	83. ___	84. ___	85. ___	86. ___	87. ___	88. ___	89. ___	90. ___	91. ___
92. ___	93. ___	94. ___	95. ___	96. ___	97. ___	98. ___	99. ___	100. ___	101. ___	102. ___	103. ___	104. ___
105. ___	106. ___	107. ___	108. ___	109. ___	110. ___	111. ___	112. ___	113. ___	114. ___	115. ___	116. ___	117. ___
118. ___	119. ___	120. ___	121. ___	122. ___	123. ___	124. ___	125. ___	126. ___	127. ___	128. ___	129. ___	130. ___

Totals:
Category: A B C D E F G H I J K L M

Grand Total: ___

Rascalinity Test Worksheet:

	A	B	C	D	E	F	G	H	I	J	K	L	M
	1. ___	2. ___	3. ___	4. ___	5. ___	6. ___	7. ___	8. ___	9. ___	10. ___	11. ___	12. ___	13. ___
	14. ___	15. ___	16. ___	17. ___	18. ___	19. ___	20. ___	21. ___	22. ___	23. ___	24. ___	25. ___	26. ___
	27. ___	28. ___	29. ___	30. ___	31. ___	32. ___	33. ___	34. ___	35. ___	36. ___	37. ___	38. ___	39. ___
	40. ___	41. ___	42. ___	43. ___	44. ___	45. ___	46. ___	47. ___	48. ___	49. ___	50. ___	51. ___	52. ___
	53. ___	54. ___	55. ___	56. ___	57. ___	58. ___	59. ___	60. ___	61. ___	62. ___	63. ___	64. ___	65. ___
	66. ___	67. ___	68. ___	69. ___	70. ___	71. ___	72. ___	73. ___	74. ___	75. ___	76. ___	77. ___	78. ___
	79. ___	80. ___	81. ___	82. ___	83. ___	84. ___	85. ___	86. ___	87. ___	88. ___	89. ___	90. ___	91. ___
	92. ___	93. ___	94. ___	95. ___	96. ___	97. ___	98. ___	99. ___	100. ___	101. ___	102. ___	103. ___	104. ___
	105. ___	106. ___	107. ___	108. ___	109. ___	110. ___	111. ___	112. ___	113. ___	114. ___	115. ___	116. ___	117. ___
	118. ___	119. ___	120. ___	121. ___	122. ___	123. ___	124. ___	125. ___	126. ___	127. ___	128. ___	129. ___	130. ___
Totals: Category:	A	B	C	D	E	F	G	H	I	J	K	L	M

Grand Total: ___

Rascalinity Test Worksheet:

	A	B	C	D	E	F	G	H	I	J	K	L	M
	1. ___	2. ___	3. ___	4. ___	5. ___	6. ___	7. ___	8. ___	9. ___	10. ___	11. ___	12. ___	13. ___
	14. ___	15. ___	16. ___	17. ___	18. ___	19. ___	20. ___	21. ___	22. ___	23. ___	24. ___	25. ___	26. ___
	27. ___	28. ___	29. ___	30. ___	31. ___	32. ___	33. ___	34. ___	35. ___	36. ___	37. ___	38. ___	39. ___
	40. ___	41. ___	42. ___	43. ___	44. ___	45. ___	46. ___	47. ___	48. ___	49. ___	50. ___	51. ___	52. ___
	53. ___	54. ___	55. ___	56. ___	57. ___	58. ___	59. ___	60. ___	61. ___	62. ___	63. ___	64. ___	65. ___
	66. ___	67. ___	68. ___	69. ___	70. ___	71. ___	72. ___	73. ___	74. ___	75. ___	76. ___	77. ___	78. ___
	79. ___	80. ___	81. ___	82. ___	83. ___	84. ___	85. ___	86. ___	87. ___	88. ___	89. ___	90. ___	91. ___
	92. ___	93. ___	94. ___	95. ___	96. ___	97. ___	98. ___	99. ___	100. ___	101. ___	102. ___	103. ___	104. ___
	105. ___	106. ___	107. ___	108. ___	109. ___	110. ___	111. ___	112. ___	113. ___	114. ___	115. ___	116. ___	117. ___
	118. ___	119. ___	120. ___	121. ___	122. ___	123. ___	124. ___	125. ___	126. ___	127. ___	128. ___	129. ___	130. ___

Totals:
Category: A ___ B ___ C ___ D ___ E ___ F ___ G ___ H ___ I ___ J ___ K ___ L ___ M ___

Grand Total: ___

Rascalinity Test Worksheet:

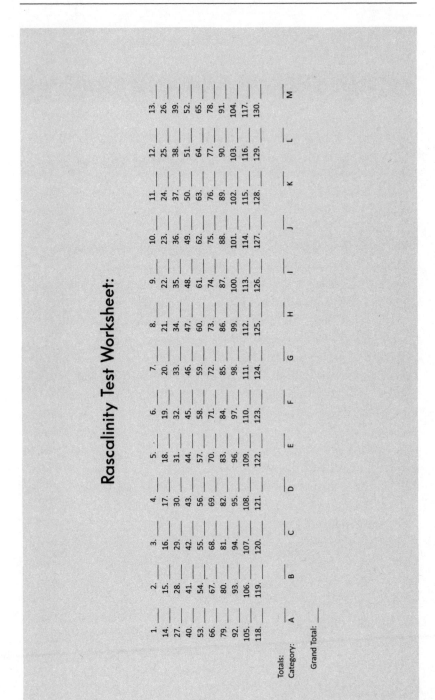

A	B	C	D	E	F	G	H	I	J	K	L	M
1. __	2. __	3. __	4. __	5. __	6. __	7. __	8. __	9. __	10. __	11. __	12. __	13. __
14. __	15. __	16. __	17. __	18. __	19. __	20. __	21. __	22. __	23. __	24. __	25. __	26. __
27. __	28. __	29. __	30. __	31. __	32. __	33. __	34. __	35. __	36. __	37. __	38. __	39. __
40. __	41. __	42. __	43. __	44. __	45. __	46. __	47. __	48. __	49. __	50. __	51. __	52. __
53. __	54. __	55. __	56. __	57. __	58. __	59. __	60. __	61. __	62. __	63. __	64. __	65. __
66. __	67. __	68. __	69. __	70. __	71. __	72. __	73. __	74. __	75. __	76. __	77. __	78. __
79. __	80. __	81. __	82. __	83. __	84. __	85. __	86. __	87. __	88. __	89. __	90. __	91. __
92. __	93. __	94. __	95. __	96. __	97. __	98. __	99. __	100. __	101. __	102. __	103. __	104. __
105. __	106. __	107. __	108. __	109. __	110. __	111. __	112. __	113. __	114. __	115. __	116. __	117. __
118. __	119. __	120. __	121. __	122. __	123. __	124. __	125. __	126. __	127. __	128. __	129. __	130. __

Totals:
Category: A   B   C   D   E   F   G   H   I   J   K   L   M

Grand Total: ___

Rascalinity Test Worksheet:

A	B	C	D	E	F	G	H	I	J	K	L	M
1. ___	2. ___	3. ___	4. ___	5. ___	6. ___	7. ___	8. ___	9. ___	10. ___	11. ___	12. ___	13. ___
14. ___	15. ___	16. ___	17. ___	18. ___	19. ___	20. ___	21. ___	22. ___	23. ___	24. ___	25. ___	26. ___
27. ___	28. ___	29. ___	30. ___	31. ___	32. ___	33. ___	34. ___	35. ___	36. ___	37. ___	38. ___	39. ___
40. ___	41. ___	42. ___	43. ___	44. ___	45. ___	46. ___	47. ___	48. ___	49. ___	50. ___	51. ___	52. ___
53. ___	54. ___	55. ___	56. ___	57. ___	58. ___	59. ___	60. ___	61. ___	62. ___	63. ___	64. ___	65. ___
66. ___	67. ___	68. ___	69. ___	70. ___	71. ___	72. ___	73. ___	74. ___	75. ___	76. ___	77. ___	78. ___
79. ___	80. ___	81. ___	82. ___	83. ___	84. ___	85. ___	86. ___	87. ___	88. ___	89. ___	90. ___	91. ___
92. ___	93. ___	94. ___	95. ___	96. ___	97. ___	98. ___	99. ___	100. ___	101. ___	102. ___	103. ___	104. ___
105. ___	106. ___	107. ___	108. ___	109. ___	110. ___	111. ___	112. ___	113. ___	114. ___	115. ___	116. ___	117. ___
118. ___	119. ___	120. ___	121. ___	122. ___	123. ___	124. ___	125. ___	126. ___	127. ___	128. ___	129. ___	130. ___

Totals:
Category: A   B   C   D   E   F   G   H   I   J   K   L   M

Grand Total: ____

About the Author

 Chris Brady earned a bachelor of science degree in mechanical engineering from Kettering University (formerly GMI) and his master of science degree in manufacturing systems engineering from Carnegie Mellon University as a General Motors Fellow. He conducted his master's thesis at Toyohashi University in Japan.

Mr. Brady co-wrote the *NY Times, Wall Street Journal, Business Weekly, USA Today,* and *Money Magazine* best seller *Launching a Leadership Revolution.* His latest book *A Month of Italy: Rediscovering the Art of Vacation* to be released in 2012 is already raved about by critics as "masterful, witty, intelligent, dreamy, and deep all at the same time." Mr. Brady also authors a highly entertaining blog (www.chrisbrady.com), was named among the Top 100 Authors to Follow on Twitter (@RascalTweets), and was selected as one of the World's Top 25 Leadership Gurus. Mr. Brady is a founder of LIFE, has been a long-term member of the Policy Council of the Team, a leadership development service provider, and has functioned as the Team's Director of All Brand Marketing since co-founding it with Orrin Woodward.

Mr. Brady is an avid motorized adventurer, pilot, world traveler, community builder, soccer fan, humorist, and historian. He also has one of the world's most unique resumes, including: experience with a live bug in his ear, walking through a paned-glass window, chickening out from the high dive in elementary school, destroying the class ant farm in third grade, losing a spelling bee on the word "use," jack-hammering his foot, and, more recently, sinking his snowmobile in a lake. Chris and his wife Terri have four children and live in both North Carolina and Florida.

LIFE
SUBSCRIPTIONS

LIFE SERIES

Our lives are lived out in the eight categories of Faith, Family, Finances, Fitness, Following, Freedom, Friendship, and Fun. The LIFE Series of 4 monthly CDs and a book is specifically designed to bring you life-transforming information in each of these categories. Whether you are interested in one or two of these areas, or all eight, you will be delighted with timeless truths and effective strategies for living a life of excellence, brought to you in an entertaining, intelligent, well-informed, and insightful manner. It has been said that it may be your life, but it's not yours to waste. Subscribe to the LIFE Series today and learn how to make yours count!

The LIFE Series – dedicated to helping people grow in each of the 8 F categories - Faith, Family, Finances, Fitness, Following, Freedom, Friendship, and Fun. 4 CDs and a book shipped each month.
$50.00 plus S&H   Pricing valid for both USD and CAD

LLR SERIES

Everyone will be called upon to lead at some point in his or her life, and often at many points. The issue is whether or not people will be ready when called. The LLR Series is based upon the *NY Times, Wall Street Journal, USA Today,* and *Money Magazine* best seller *Launching a Leadership Revolution*, written by Chris Brady and Orrin Woodward, in which leadership is taught in a way that applies to everyone. Whether you are seeking corporate or business advancement, community influence, church impact, or better stewardship and effectiveness in your home, the principles and specifics taught in the LLR Series will equip you with what you need.

The subscriber will receive 4 CDs and a leadership book each month. Topics covered will include finances, leadership, public speaking, attitude, goal setting, mentoring, game planning, accountability and tracking of progress, levels of motivation, levels of influence, and leaving a personal legacy.

Subscribe to the LLR Series and begin applying these life-transforming truths to your life today!

The LLR (Launching a Leadership Revolution) Series – dedicated to helping people grow in their leadership ability. 4 CDs and a book shipped each month. $50.00 plus S&H   Pricing valid for both USD and CAD

Don't Miss Out on the 3 for FREE Program!

As a customer or Member subscribes to any one or more of the packages, that person is given the further incentive to attract other customers who subscribe as well. Once that customer or Member signs up three or more customers on equivalent or greater dollar value subscriptions, the customer or Member will get his or her next month's subscription FREE!

AGO SERIES

Whether you have walked with Christ your entire life or have just begun the journey, we welcome you to experience the love, joy, understanding, and purpose that only Christ can offer. This series is designed to touch and nourish the hearts of all faith levels as our top speakers, along with special guest speakers, help you enhance your understanding of God's plan for your life, your marriage, your children, and your character, while providing valuable support and guidance needed by all Christians. Nurture your soul, strengthen your faith, and find answers on the go or quietly at home with the AGO Series.

The AGO (All Grace Outreach) Series – dedicated to helping people grow spiritually. 1 CD and a book shipped each month.
$25.00 plus S&H
Pricing valid for both USD and CAD

EDGE SERIES

Designed especially for those on the younger side of life, the Edge Series is a hard-core, no frills approach to learning the things that will make for a successful life.

Eliminate the noise around you about who you are and who you should become. Instead, figure it out for yourself in a mighty way with life-changing information from people who would do just about anything to have learned these truths much, much sooner in life! It may have taken them a lifetime to discover these truths, but what they learned can be yours now on a monthly basis.

Edge Series – dedicated to helping young people grow.
1 CD shipped each month.
$10.00 plus S&H
Pricing valid for both USD and CAD